A VINEYARD IN
TUSCANY

ALSO BY

FERENC MÁTÉ

FROM A BARE HULL
THE WORLD'S BEST SAILBOATS
A REASONABLE LIFE
THE HILLS OF TUSCANY
GHOST SEA
A NEW ENGLAND AUTUMN

A VINEYARD IN
TUSCANY

A WINE LOVER'S DREAM

FERENC MÁTÉ

W.W. NORTON   NEW YORK   LONDON

ISBN 978-0-920256-56-5

The text in this book is composed in Adobe Garamond

Book design and composition by Candace Máté
Manufactured by R. R. Donnelley, U. S. A.

Albatross Books at
W. W. Norton & Company Inc., 500 Fifth Avenue, New York, NY 10110
www.wwnorton.com

W. W. Norton & Company Ltd., Castle House, 75/76 Wells Street, London W1T 3QT
1 2 3 4 5 6 7 8 9 0

For Candace and Buster

And our dear friend
Carlo Corino

Contents

A VINEYARD IN
TUSCANY

1 ~ THE SODDISFAZIONE

*P*aolucci and I sat on his worn stone steps, bread and prosciutto in one hand, a glass of red wine in the other—it was an hour before lunch—and looked between the cypresses, across the valley to the hill town of Montepulciano. The bells swung in the steeple and filled the noonday with their song. Rosanna came out of the vineyard, perspiring in the heat, and put her hoe, headfirst, into a bucket of water to keep the wood from drying. With her sleeve, she wiped the sweat from her eyes, and then went into the kitchen to stir the simmering wild boar *in umido*.

"Don't worry, Rosa," Paolucci said. "When I win the lottery, things will be different."

"I'll have a new hoe handle?" Rosanna taunted.

"There'll be no more hoes!" Paolucci retorted. "No hoeing and no pruning, and no more tying the *maledetti* vines. No more worry about fungus and mildew, or too much rain or drought. You'll just take it easy and I'll just drink more wine."

"More than now?" asked Rosanna. "You'll have to do it in your sleep."

Paolucci drank. "I pray to God there's no afterlife," he grumbled. "If there is, she'll bust my balls until the end of time."

He refilled our glasses. "You don't want a vineyard, Francesco," he said. "You don't want a wife either but it's too late for that—but it's not too late to *not* get a vineyard. A vineyard is like a grave; the dead man in it can never leave the ground."

"But the *soddisfazione*?" I asked.

"Here's the *soddisfazione*!" he said, holding up his glass. "I'll give you all the *soddisfazione* you can drink. Why ruin your life?"

He might as well have been talking to the stones.

As I walked home after lunch, all I could think of was having my own vines.

Our house sat below the ridge, a quarter mile down the dusty road from Paolucci's. It was called La Marinaia, the sailor's wife, and why it had that name sixty miles from the sea God only knows—the neighbors certainly didn't, and not a single one of them lost sleep over it.

The house had been restored a few years back with heavy oak beams in the ceilings and hand-made terracotta floors. The ground floor—once stables—was now a long entrance with plenty of room for books, a pantry a few steps down, and a kitchen opposite with a fireplace and glass doors to the garden. The dining room was fit for royal declarations and the living room had a fireplace big enough to roast the village sow. Upstairs were three bedrooms with views of Montepulciano to break an opera-set designer's heart.

The surrounding gardens had been a Pharaonic task for the previous owner, a financier. The hills around Montepulciano are mostly clay, so good dirt had to be imported for the cypresses, laurel, lavender, and rosemary. The financier shrewdly planted a grove of walnuts to be sold in twenty years for high-class lumber to pad his coffers, but in the hard clay they barely grew, and weren't even fit for toothpicks when he died.

Though the house sat in an ocean of fields and vines, only two acres belonged to us, and on it we planted the essential: fifty man-height olives.

To own a vineyard I would have to buy more land.

~

I walked past Paolucci's vines, past the reedy pond where wild ducks nested, and past the Talosa vineyard that almost touched our house. A loud-mouthed Roman ran it. Over the years he had swindled every neighbor out of something, and I had once heard the banker across the creek yell after him, "you're lucky this isn't Sicily, because then you would be dead!"

I stared at the rows of vines curving down the hill, the

young buds swelling on pruned stalks, and the freshly fur-
rowed ground awaiting rain. I dreamt of my own vineyard,
full of the bustle of *vendemmia*, the grape harvest, interrupted at noon for great meals at long tables under the bowers
before walking back into the vineyards, tipsy and smiling, the
shears now cutting the *grappoli* twice as fast. Then I dreamt
of the weeks in the cellar during fermentation, that intoxicating sweet smell filling the air and following you out into
the star-filled night. And the long winter evenings, thinking
of the full oak barrels where the wine slept, aging slowly.

And then I dreamt of the very best part: a bottle, on the
table cloth, reflecting candlelight, and our dinner guests staring in admiration at the elegant label of our very own wine.

2 ~ THE VINEYARD NEXT DOOR

*T*uscans hate Romans. And it's not just from a two-thousand -year-old feud when, as D. H. Lawrence wrote, "the Romans, in their usual neighborly fashion, wiped out . . . the Etruscan existence as a nation and a people . . . the inevitable result of expansion with a big E, which is the sole *raison d'être* of people like the Romans." Nor is it just because medieval armies of the velvet-robed Popes spent inordinate amounts of time trying to subjugate Tuscany. To the contrary, the Tuscans appreciate the unique Roman Catholic contribution to their culture: the *bestemmia*, swearing. The *bestemmia* by definition involves Popes, saints, priests, and above all La Madonna, coupled with pigs, dogs, wolves, snakes, and other wild and domestic beasts in creative positions that would make a pretzel-maker proud.

The present disdain is primarily because Tuscans, whose *parole sono d'oro*, or word is gold, have found through bitter experience that Romans are too often shifty, shameless crooks.

I tried to buy the vineyard next door from the most shameless of them all.

In most countries, starting a vineyard is no big deal; you go out back, stick a few sprouting vine shoots in the ground, and there you are. But not in Tuscany. The region is tightly controlled, so converting a wheat field or pasture into vines is a bureaucratic minefield. The controls are most draconian in the DOCG (Denominazione di Origine Controllata e Garantita) zones of Chianti Classico, Vino Nobile di Montepulciano, and that world-coveted, *Wine Spectator*'s 2006 Wine of the Year: Brunello di Montalcino. DOCG's grapes must be planted within defined boundaries of the zone; cross the road or extend beyond the ditch and you've gone too far. The DOCG also controls the yield per acre and the amount of wine. Furthermore, to prevent fraud, the wine cannot leave the zone for any reason until it is bottled and labeled. In fact, the Fraud Squad, *I Frodi*, swoops down on wineries unannounced and makes you account for every last drop of wine. Except of course for the few cases they take away as bribes.

The boundary of each pasture, vineyard, olive grove, and wood is noted on a master map called *il catasto*, a close kin of "catastrophe"; the etymology is evident when you look at the countryside. There isn't a straight line in all of Tuscany. How and why, through thousands of years, the twisting and turning boundaries and odd nooks and crannies came to be defined staggers even the most imaginative mind. Yes, sometimes crests of hills or creeks make obvious confines, but just as often it seems the line swerved to include a tree or rock, or because a hen was brooding under a certain bush just then, or because of where great-grandmother made her special offerings to the parish priest.

Now, to change the "use" of any field to a vineyard requires something just short of a Papal Decree. First, you must buy planting rights. These are available only from those who have uprooted their own old and (of course) *catasto*-registered vines. Why, you might ask, would anyone do that? The obvious answer is to sell the rights. But most often these sellers are small, sustenance-type farmers with only a few hundred vines, so to compile a whole acre's worth you might have to find four or five farmers. Trying to maximize their gain, they will sell only under the table to avoid paying taxes on it all. Like many things in Tuscany, these affairs are done through intermediaries who make certain that the sellers and buyers never meet. This is so the intermediary can play both ends against the middle, the middle being himself where most of the cash ends up. Yes, I said cash. It's not unusual to see a suitcase stuffed with bills during one of these transactions, and since all of this is done on the sly, there are of course no receipts. This is why a Tuscan's word had to be as good as gold; otherwise, there would be bloodletting every day. And this is why I should never have tried to deal with a Roman.

~

One corner of the vineyard above us nearly touched our brick *piazzetta* that was cut into the hillside. Candace, our son Peter and I spent most warm summer nights there eating and drinking at the marble table under the grape arbor, and I sat there many a hot summer afternoon staring at the vineyard, dreaming it would one day be mine. The vineyard wasn't large, just over three acres, but it would yield about 8,000 bottles per year, certainly enough to start a small winery. And it wasn't greed or romantic dreaming that drove me—it had more to do with the fact that as a writer I don't have a pension, and even though I was still only in my forties, it would be reassuring to think that when I was too old for globetrotting, I'd be able to fall back on the income from a vineyard of our own.

The vineyard itself was a mess. It was owned by a Roman consortium, as were others in the valley. These investment groups are seldom held together by knowledge of wine and they hire an administrator to bring in maximum returns. Passion for the countryside or vineyards has no place in such an operation. The corporate vineyards, like the one above us, are often weed-choked until they need to be carpet-bombed with herbicides. New shoots hang every which way, untrimmed, and over-fertilized to produce gargantuan grape clusters without much flavor, finesse, or perfume. The poles are often broken and askew, and the soil is either seldom tilled or it's tilled at the wrong time, because those who own the vineyards just don't give a damn.

In direct contrast are vineyards owned *and* worked by those who love them. Here vines tend to look more like specimens from a Kyoto garden: pruned with care, the weeds hoed by hand or with a painfully slow mechanical plow that goes in and out among the stalks to extract the greedy weeds. Double green pruning—costly in time spent and in grapes lost—is the norm, leaving only one cluster of grapes per shoot to concentrate flavors.

The vineyard above us was like an old, abandoned ruin just waiting for love and care to bring it back to life.

~

"I think I'll go put in an offer on the vineyard," I said to Candace, who was reading in the late afternoon light.

She looked at me like a mother whose son has just announced he wanted to be the Virgin Mary.

"That's nice, dear," she sighed.

"I heard they sell for ten thousand bucks an acre."

"Chump change."

"We can convert the underground garage into a cellar."

"Why not."

"Look. Petrus has only a couple acres, just like this— all clay, just like this—and the owners are bloody millionaires."

She didn't even sigh.

Encouraged by her silence I blurted, full of joy, "What should we call it?"

She put down her book and took off her glasses. "How about, 'Ralph Cramden's Wines.'"

~

I barely slept that night.

Early the next morning I was on my way trotting up the dirt road to meet the Roman administrator in his cellars near the top of Montepulciano. I slowed as I passed Paolucci, to tell him where I was going and why.

"You want vines? Take mine!" he shouted after me.

"I want them next to my house," I smiled.

"Fine. I'll chainsaw the bastards and bring them in the cart!"

It was always good to have an excuse to go to town. I'd walk the dirt road to the base of the hill, then zigzag up past the cemetery, past the beautiful Renaissance temple of San Biagio, with its travertine walls and tower starkly white against the green slope, then climb and climb to the massive walls of the town and look back at the rolling countryside far below. In its middle, like a ship in a sea of green, stood our house, La Marinaia, the perfect dream. Except for the damned vineyard so tempting beside it.

Talosa's cellars made me flush with envy. They were deep caverns hewed out of the sandstone hill by the Etruscans millennia ago, and behind Talosa's wrought iron gate were enormous oak casks full of wine nestled in the musky gloom. The Roman, all smiles, threw his shapeless form at me in greeting, patted my back, and talked to me as loudly as if I were standing across the valley.

"Rumor has it," he roared, "that you'd like to buy a vineyard." Talosa had over a hundred acres of vines scattered around Montepulciano. He dug out an old map and a copy of the *catasto*, checked the measure, and grinned.

"I have a perfect one for you—a ten-minute drive from your house. West exposure so the grapes won't cook. Two acres, not too steep. The going price is ten thousand dollars per acre, but because we're friends, I'll make it nine."

I was shocked. And I felt awful for having thought badly of him. I thanked him but said I what I really wanted was the one beside our house. It wasn't just for show, I told him, but that we didn't like his use of herbicides. I, on the other hand, planned to run an organic vineyard.

He smiled. And I could have sworn he licked his chops.

"I understand how you feel," he said. "I don't like it either, I would do organic too, but the owners . . . I have to stay alive."

"The vineyard is a bit abandoned," I appealed. "It needs new poles, some new vines, new ditches. But with a little work I think I can . . . "

"Sure you can," he smiled. "But to be really honest, those vines are old," he said. "Another ten years and they have to be replanted. So I'll give you a special price."

I restrained myself from kissing both his cheeks.

"It could be another Petrus," he smiled, seeing my excitement.

"Well, I don't think right away," I lied.

"With your brains and that land, it'll take no time at all."

I should have smelled a rat. And if not right then, surely when he backed out of reach and slumped behind his desk. He twitched a bit, looked at the map, and punched his calculator.

"Shall I tell you in lira or in U. S. dollars?" he drooled.

I didn't give a damn if it was in Russian rubles, I just wanted to hear the price. I imagined if the other was nine thousand per acre for a vineyard in good shape, good exposure, then this one, old, steep, and needing a lot of work—*plus* we were neighbors, he had said "friends"—would be more like seven.

He took out a piece of paper, scribbled and pushed it over to me. "There you are," he shouted. "An official, special, between-friends price. On paper. Even signed."

I looked. I couldn't believe my eyes. How could have I thought badly of him? He was a true friend. And more, a remarkable gentleman, the kind they don't make anymore. I thought all that with moist eyes because on the paper before me danced the number 5.

"I'll get the cash by the end of . . . " The cellar started spinning. I felt hot. As I was speaking, I looked past the 5 at the endless stream of zeros.

"Fifty thousand?" I sputtered.

"Dollari Americani," he answered and laughed so loud the barrels shook.

"But you said, 'friends,'" I pleaded.

"Best friends," he chimed. "If we weren't, I'd want a hundred. So for you, it's only fifty."

"But the other was only nine."

He pushed the map in front of me and leaned close, like a wolf staring a chicken in the eye.

"That one is there," he said as he poked a blunt finger at the map's distant edge. "And this other one is here. Right beside your house."

I was out of air.

"Come on," he smiled. "What's fifty thousand an acre when you'll make a million with your new Petrus tomorrow?"

I sat there speechless. Any decent businessman would have argued, reasoned, made a counter offer, retorted. Instead I was busy deciding whether to rip the stone sink from the wall and beat him with it, or squish his toad body into the toilet and flush.

I went to leave. At the door, I remembered the banker's words about Sicily. I turned. "You don't have a vineyard near Palermo we could see?"

He giggled nervously and crumpled in his chair to make a smaller target.

But fate was kind. Within a few short months, I was offered sweet revenge.

3 ~ OUR TUSCAN LIFE

*H*ungarians thrive on adversity. Our chances of winning are
multiplied tenfold if we start dead last, and while it may seem
as though we're often too busy drinking and dancing to take
notice, we can only be pushed so far—as the Russians found
out to their chagrin with the 1956 Revolution. It's not that
we're belligerent or hard to get along with, but you have to
be wary of a people that has remained unadulterated for a
thousand years without forbidding natural boundaries to
prevent intermingling. The only logical explanation I've heard
is my grandmother's: "Who'd marry a Hungarian if they
didn't have to?"

By the time I sipped my second scotch in Andrew's tall
and skinny house overlooking the valley, I had my plan,
although had I been wise I would have followed Andrew's
example. He's a fine painter and sculptor from England—
Wordsworth was his great great something or other whose
writing desk Andrew still has—who manages to live and

work in Tuscany *and* enjoy it. And he finds time to travel because of a simple fact: he owns no land. Or, to be precise: his house covers every inch of the land he owns. His three-story *palazzotto* is on the very edge of town. When I say edge, I mean it's atop the great wall that encircles Montepulciano, the wall that here, on the Northwest side, sits on a sandstone cliff with woods and the cemetery down below. His sculpture studio and wine cellar are on the bottom floor, his painting studio and kitchen on the next, and the bedrooms up above. It's full of sunlight and on a good clear day he can see all the way to China. When he's fed up with it all, he packs his car, closes the shutters, and off he goes for indefinite sojourns to Greece, Spain, Sicily or the Moon. Why could I not learn from his contentment? What curse drove me to want more? More *land*, of all things!

Andrew listened patiently to my ranting, but instead of advice, he brought over a paper bag from the baker, full of fresh, still-warm focaccia. He poured olive oil into a little bowl and pushed it in front of me as if he were trying to calm a cat. "Eat," he said. "You'll feel better if you eat."

Baked into the focaccia were bits of olives and some crumbled rosemary. Either the bread or the murky olive oil soothed me. Or was it the sixteen-year-old Islay single malt?

~

Through the window I saw swallows dive and soar in the updraft from the walls. I had made up my mind: we were moving. We would sell the house, encircled and besieged by the toad's fields, and buy a ruin with a vineyard.

Here I must confess another weakness. All my life I had wanted to rebuild a ruin. At the age of five, on sunny Sunday mornings, I would cross the Danube with my Grandfather to gather wildflowers in the hills of Buda for Grandma. I remember seeing the crumbling wall of an ancient watch-tower and dreaming about it for the rest of the week: how to re-fit stones, put in new beams, and be lord and master of my very own castle. I never outgrew the dream.

La Marinaia had robbed me of these joys. It had been so perfectly done, garden and all, that the only thing that remained for me was mowing the lawn (possibly the dullest task God ever assigned).

I awaited Andrew's advice on my plan, but he just shook his head, smiled, and filled my glass again. When, after the glass was empty, I still insisted on following through, he said, "Don't sell until you've eaten. Life looks different after lunch."

On the way home, I stopped in the Duomo in Piazza Grande at the top of town to clear my head and seek the Madonna's advice. Hanging in a small frame, she's from *il quattrocento*—painted on wood, holding her baby. A dark blue sky is behind her and she has an enigmatic expression that, depending on the light, could be seen as encouraging or chiding. The Duomo was, as it almost always is, without a living soul. The soft light came through the clerestory win-dows and lit the dreary cardinals on the marble floors. The Madonna was waiting. I stood below her, grinning from the scotch, but that didn't seem to bother her. As I told her the day's events, her face darkened, and just as I got to the word "vineyard," outright laughter rang from the walls and echoed in the dome. The front doors opened and in rushed a group of schoolchildren wearing backpacks. They swarmed about while I stood there without her final answer. Unless, of course, it was the children's laughter.

~

When we bought La Marinaia, I was sure that I would leave it only when they carried me out feet first. Yet here I was, with the prospect of changing houses putting a spring in my step on the way home—admittedly it was downhill. The one thing I felt bad about was telling Paolucci. To avoid that task for now, I took a back road, cut through vineyards and along a field of poppies—there are no fences in Tuscany unless you're trying to keep in sheep—and crossed the creek, climbed our hill, and ended up at the house.

Candace was—as she always is—in her vegetable garden, hoeing. She hoes day or night, rain or shine, seasons be damned. Years later our son described her to all of Grandma's birthday guests as "My Mom the Great: great cooker, great runner, and great hoer." Grandma laughed until she cried. The men raised their eyebrows.

"The toad wanted a usurious price," I said. "So I think we should get out of here and find a place with more land."

"That's nice, dear," she sighed.

"I mean it."

17

"Of course you do. You always do. But you'll feel better after lunch."

There are certain things in life that women don't understand. What they do seem to understand, and only too bloody well, is how to use words as knives. Which is why women never fight a war. They don't need to. With few words they can lay waste to an adversary faster than a salami slicer. And it comes to them effortlessly, in fact often trimmed with glee. "And what did Paolucci say when you told him?" the Great Hoer asked.

~

The Paoluccis truly were family. Or, more precisely, they had adopted us.

Not only had they patiently taught us Italian, but they had advised with every aspect of working the land. They also helped us plant the vegetable garden, prune and take care of our fruit trees, berry bushes, figs, and olives, and they even showed us how to hunt for *porcini* and chanterelles. Most Sundays we were expected for their family feast where, more often then not, we were the only guests. There we would gorge ourselves from noon onward, starting with assorted crostini, toasted bread dressed with mushrooms or liver paste or tomatoes. We would move on to two different pastas, lasagna with *sugo, ravioli con funghi, pinci al cinghiale,* or wild boar, followed by wood-oven roasted Guinea hen or duck, and long ribs grilled by the fire, or veal stuffed with sausages or ham and mushrooms or apples. Finally, the sweets: some soaked in grappa, others like *tiramisù* heaped with cream, and just before your heart gave out, a violent espresso to kick it back to life.

Evenings they or we would drop by and sit around the fireplace together, dipping our *biscottini*, a hard-baked biscuit with nuts, into our vin santo, an aged sweet wine as rich and powerful as sherry. We'd chat or play cards, or watch the kids do homework or Nonna, Paolucci's mom, knit wool socks. We were together for the holidays: Christmas, Easter, the Annunciation, Liberation, and all those other "ations" the Italians fill the year with, all marked with feasts. And in a most moving gesture, their daughter Carla's wedding was rescheduled from summer to fall, because we had to be in Vancouver in July for a blood-family event.

We tried our best to reciprocate. In June we helped rake the long rows of hay, and pitched and stored it for the cows in winter. We helped throughout the year with the vines: pruning in January, tying the shoots in May, and with the *vendemmia* in October. In the spring we pruned olives, in November we helped pick them, and in the dead of winter we went down to the creek to cut firewood, roast sausages, and drink wine to keep warm, then we hauled the wood home with the tractor through the mud. And, on a cold day before Christmas, we turned the fattened sow into sausages, prosciutto, salami, and pork chops.

But more binding than their connection to us was their love for our son Peter, whom we endearingly call Buster. They didn't so much embrace him as confiscate him. The girls,

Eleanora and Carla, both in their teens, dragged him every-where like a big doll. They took him shopping, swimming, for walks, and sometimes even on their dates. Rosanna and Nonna played it a bit cooler, although once when he was in their kitchen they simply shut the door and fussed over him. Rosanna taught him to cook. He stirred, kneaded, and rolled, but, most of all, he ate everything at each stage of cooking. Nonna knitted him so many socks and gloves that every sheep in the valley must have shivered through those winters. Every day he would go with her to the attic to flip and salt the curing hams. He would help her in the vegetable garden, or feeding the chickens and searching the shrubs for hidden eggs, or rounding up her wandering sow.

As soon as he was old enough, not yet five, Paolucci had him in his lap while driving the tractor and on his saddle while riding his horse. He sat with him for hours in the warm, sweet-smelling stable, while Buster stared at his four cows, calf, and goat with as much concentration as if he were counting each hair on their bodies. When the vet brought over a tiny lamb that wouldn't nurse from his mother, Paolucci milked one of his cows, poured the milk into a baby bottle, and let Buster go with a rubber nipple and play mamma to the lamb. At *vendemmia*, he was on the cart with another neighbor, Bazzotti, emptying the pickers' baskets, then at the cantina he pounded and crushed the grapes with a pestle as big as he was.

So telling the Paoluccis we were moving would be like telling unsuspecting parents that their children were leaving home.

~

In addition to lacking a vineyard and being too close to someone else's, La Marinaia had another drawback: there were no woods to speak of. I have always thought woods to be a quintessential part of country life, not just for firewood but also for the smells, colors, animals, and mystery—and of course—*porcini*.

We were also just a bit too close to town; my idea of happiness is dangling my feet off the edge of the earth. Plus it was small. Houseguests often took over my cramped office and Candace had nowhere to paint. She tried the big dining room but the smell of her oils made even the best dinners taste of turpentine. She did, finally, find herself a studio in a secluded part of Montepulciano and along with it a beau: Vittorio, the last country-town gentleman of his kind.

Vittorio was in his golden age, lean, gentle, and impeccably dressed even if he was just walking to the baker. In Tuscany this is no small undertaking, as one is forced to stop every ten feet for some *chiacchiera*, gossip, either with other town folk running their daily errands or with shopkeepers who dally before their shops to hear the latest rumors. Besides the inevitable topic of weather, this included the latest on the neighbors: who married whom, who left whom, who was driving off into the country with you know who right behind.

Vittorio lived in an alley of winding steps edged with a garden; hence there were no cars, and the only noise was gossip from the windows. He owned a vast space next door to his house with windows that looked onto the mysterious garden of a convent. The space had once housed a printing shop but now stood empty. Candace was thrilled—the rent was only $50 a month, whereas in New York she had paid $400 for a hole so dark and dank that the mushroom-grower tenant before her had called the Health Department. Vittorio hesitated because he thought the space was too grim, unbefitting an artist; the walls were shedding plaster, the cement floor chipped, and the old beams overhead painted with tar, but the windows and doors opened and closed and there was even a toilet: a ceramic hole in the floor that had once been white. Finally Vittorio agreed, but only if we gave him a month to have it cleaned.

When we returned to see the space, after the clean-up, we walked right by it; it was unrecognizable. The outside had been painted, doors and windows sanded and varnished, lace curtains hung, and there were pots of blooming geraniums in the windows. Inside, the walls had been replastered and were sparkling white, the floor was now of new ceramic tiles, and the ceiling had been sandblasted, its oak beams restained. The space where the hole had been was now an enclosed, white-tiled bathroom with a toilet, bidet, sink and a shower.

"More suited to an artist," Vittorio said softly.

Candace gave him a suspiciously long hug.

That studio, too, would be another victim of my dream.

4 ~ RUIN-HUNTING

*F*ew things in life are as wonderful as spending lazy after-noons in the hills of Tuscany looking for a ruin. The dream zone is surprisingly small, from Montepulciano north to Trequanda, west to Massa Marittima, then south to Pitigliano. I covered so much of it by bike, car, and on foot that farmers began to recognize and address me as Il Cercatore: The Searcher.

Much of this area is wild, with dense forests or rugged mountain pastures, with few houses and only narrow roads twisting through valleys or on ridges. At sunset or in winter mist, its sea of hills will take your breath away. Below the forests, most of the countryside is a mix of olive groves, wheat fields, and vines.

I began modestly, heading on foot into the hills behind the house. Most of the land here, all the way to Pienza, is owned by Sardinian shepherds who came in the 1960s when land was cheap and government grants flowed like water. The zone has since become famous for *pecorino*, a richly flavored sheep cheese made into small rounds, which is especially good fresh—just a couple of weeks old when it's soft, white, and mild—or aged up to four months, when it tastes rich and piquant and is as dense as *parmigiano*.

The sheep farms are large—sheep devour every blade of grass so they need considerable pastures—and passing through them on foot is easy once you find a gate or climb the fence. This is heaven for ruin hunters, as large tracts are owned by only one family, and very few stone *poderi*, houses, have been restored.

I cut through a field—the sheep glared but kept eating—and I walked down into a wooded gully and found my first ruin, an ancient, abandoned mill. No house could have held more mystery. Nestled in a shady hollow in the cleft of two hills, it was surrounded by a wood of oaks and poplars. Fed by the stream, they had grown majestic over the centuries. Behind the small house was a windowless stone shed. I entered through the only opening, a low doorway, and waited for my eyes to grow used to the gloom. The light spread feebly through the empty space. The shed was in fact an enormous, brick-lined cistern, its ceilings arched to create a long tunnel. Water had been stored here to keep the mill's wheels turning when the stream ran low. What a place this could be to write, to let loose your imagination in the silence and half-light, and what a cool place all summer long when the merciless Tuscan sun plundered the open valley. I sat in a silence so complete my ears rang until I heard footsteps on the stone walk up above. It was Bonari the pig farmer from nearby. He was casting into a tiny pond behind the dam. We exchanged *buonaseras* but eyed each other, each with the conviction that the other was crazy.

"You think you're going to catch fish in that puddle?" I scoffed.

"You think you can survive in that dank hole?" he retorted.

"Quiet and cool. A good place to live."

He looked into the damp shadows, then shrugged his shoulders. "If you're a rat."

One should not go ruin-hunting sober. It's best to start out right after lunch with the sun high, your stomach full, and your brain alight with wine. The wine is not just good for disposition, but with it you don't give a damn how far you walk, what walls you scale, or how the brambles claw your thighs. And even though you'll have a burning desire to possess some arch, some long view, or a charming attic, you'll also forget it faster once the wine wears off. And the *contadini* you'll meet in the fields along the way are likely to feel as rosy as you, so you'll make fast friends and be invited to hear stories about the old days. They might tell you of some secret spot in the woods or on a hilltop where your ruin is hidden. Of course sometimes there is no ruin and you might get stuck chatting for hours, or, as in one case—when the farmer heard I wrote books—listening to his endless and deadly poetry.

Day by day I enlarged my circle. I found intriguing houses but on barren hilltops, where the *tramontana* wind of winter would blow you off your feet, or the summer sun roast you from dawn 'til dusk, where it would take decades in the hard clay to grow trees to fend wind or give you shade. I also found *poderi* in beautiful locations notched into hillsides, or between two hills, but they were either the size of a shoebox or ruins whose roofs had caved in and walls barely stood, meaning they would have to be torn down and built anew.

What complicated the search was my insistence on vines. By the time I drifted toward Pienza, only eight miles to the west, I had entered a zone of stifling heat and rock-hard *tufo*, sandstone, in which the vines would never thrive.

On drizzly days I took the Matra, an old French sports car made of fiberglass thin as an eggshell with a steel frame about as robust as a paperclip. It is, however, wonderfully stable, being almost as wide as it is long—it has three seats side by side—and is slung so low it has trouble making it over freshly painted lines. On winding Tuscan roads it is a dream, for it handles like a go-cart and its potent mid-engine blasts you out of curves.

But once you're on the dirt roads that dominate this region, you'll find yourself scraping and banging with a dreadful clamor. Any reasonable person would avoid such rough byways—unless he was born Hungarian, hence never taught the word "no." So when a ruin displayed itself on a distant hill, I put my foot down and the Matra scraped and banged until, with a deafening blow, it stopped dead with the engine still revving. In the middle of nowhere, without a house in sight, we sat there. It was getting dark; I cursed in Hungarian. This was time consuming, as we are the cursing champions of the world, as proven at an international swear-off, where my victorious compatriot managed an entire half hour without repeating a single term. He even beat the Tuscans.

I swore so long I ran out of breath. And light.

Crawling under the car I expected to see the transmission lying on the ground, but there was nothing on the ground except a few hundred ants and a dangling rod that used to shift the gears. All I could do was make more loud suggestions to the Saints.

"Buonasera," a gentle voice said. I pulled my head out from under the car. I didn't have to look too far. A tiny old lady stood dressed in classic Tuscan garb: a thin dress and an apron. She held a tall stick and was surrounded by curious sheep. I explained the problem and she smiled.

"My house is nearby," she said, "and there is light. Maybe my husband can help you fix your car."

I looked around, but saw no house.

"A long way to push," I said.

"No push," she said. "Pull."

Nothing is more embarrassing than three rams, side by side, pulling your sports car on a rope.

⌐

I widened my search. My favorite valley, around Petroio, was tiny and had no land for vines. Monte Amiata, the looming volcano, was too high and cold for grapes. The lowlands toward the sea had no ancient ruins because until only recently they were malarial swamps, so whoever got started building a house didn't get far before he died.

The area around Siena, arguably the most beautiful city in Tuscany, was too hot and dry. Besides, it had a horror you could not hide from: a giant silo of steel and concrete twenty stories high, abandoned and crumbling. Tearing it down would cost too much, so it stands to this day in the glorious green valley as a permanent monument to imbecility. It was a government project to develop a poor region. The Siena hills are hard, unrelenting clay where only the strongest of grains had been planted, until someone decided to turn the valley into the largest source of Italy's national vegetable: the tomato. Everyone cheered, the cranes arrived, and the silo and a cannery around it appeared overnight. There were brass band parades and feasts. They planted the tomatoes; a few hundred acres of tiny shoots bobbed in the warm breeze, but within a week the valley of fresh green shoots had turned uniformly brown; every single one had shriveled up and died, all because someone forgot that the hills of Siena lack the one thing that tomatoes need: water. The only ripe tomatoes the silo ever saw were those the guard brought with him in his lunch every day.

I quit. There wasn't a tree in Tuscany I hadn't looked behind.

Don't judge me impatient; I'm talking months. I didn't start again until the following spring, when Italy was in a dragnet of a judicial manhunt *mani pulite*, clean hands. The leading federal judge decided to clamp down on all bribes, so many who the day before had flaunted their wealth became suspiciously dirt-poor overnight. Ferraris and Maseratis vanished off the streets, beach houses and ski chalets were shuttered from coast to coast, fur coats disappeared and women shivered, and sticky-fingered bureaucrats were gasping from mowing their own lawns.

It was a calm day at La Marinaia. After a morning of writing, Buster and I were playing soccer in the field behind the house. He blasted the ball so hard with his muscular little legs—he spent hours every day pedaling his toy tractor through the hills—that the walls of the house shook each time his cannonade shot by me.

Candace was helping Eleanora with her English homework under the arbor when she called out, "Chum, I think I found your dream."

I froze. Buster blasted and La Marinaia trembled. I went to look. They'd been practicing English by reading an Italian *Country House* magazine, which had a photograph atop each page, with two columns of print below. One in Italian, the other in English. I stared at the photo and couldn't believe my eyes. It was an aerial shot of a small, enchanted castle. It looked long abandoned; the olives around it were overrun with brambles, broom drowned the fruit trees, the forest that came down the hill seemed an impenetrable jungle, and a nearby hayloft had completely collapsed.

But the house, my God the house. It must have been built over many centuries. Bits and pieces were added everywhere—the roofs angled in various directions—and doors and windows were all at different heights as if the ground level had changed, or ideas had changed, as generations came and went. Two wings—two stories high, one shed-roofed the other gabled-formed between them what I had dreamed of all these years: a courtyard. Past the wings, the house spread massively, and from it rose that rare gem: a tower. The heading read: Potential wine estate, Tuscany.

I broke out in a sweat. "I need a drink," I said.

"Dad, come play ball," Buster yelled.

"Dad's legs won't move, darling," Candace said. She poured me a glass of wine. "You had better sit down," she said, concerned, "before I read you the rest."

"In Italy's most prestigious wine zone, Montalcino, a rare opportunity for a wine estate for the most discerning. Nestled in the side of one of two private hills is a five thousand square-foot, 13-century friary. Fabulous form, ready for your imaginative restoration. Surrounded by 70 acres of land: forests, olives, fields, and a small vineyard. Thirty acres of the land is ideal for vines. Five acres of planting rights for Brunello di Montalcino included." And lastly the price.

Candace refilled my glass. "Don't stop breathing now, Chum," she said. "We're expected for dinner."

I walked back to the soccer field. Bang, the ball blasted by.

"Dad," Buster chided, "It's no fun if you don't move ."

5 ~ THE THIRTEEN BEST

*T*he road from Montepulciano to Montalcino is a sports car fanatic's dream. There are 240 curves, or, to put it simply, you are turning the entire time, for in those twenty-five miles there are only three straight bits longer than fifty yards. This is no challenge if you putter at the posted speed limit of about 40 mph, but trying to hit 100 gets your attention.

Past San Biagio and its avenue of cypresses, the road turns west between small fields and olive groves and then down the hill to a two-hundred-yard stretch. If you anticipate well, you can hit 100 by the end, then you brake until the discs smoke because here come the real curves. You climb through blind curves past the Cucuzi's sheep and run the ridge all the way to Pienza straightening the curves by using both sides of the road (and a bit of grass along the ditch because you learned in grade six from Miss McClelland that the shortest distance between two points is always a straight line).

Coming out of the curves, 60 feels just right. Until you spot the *carabinieri*, the national police, armed to the teeth at the turn-off to Petroio. They come smiling in their bullet-proof vests, Uzis wobbling in casual Italian fashion, finger on the trigger so they won't have to waste time when they decide to turn your car into a sieve. You learn quickly that all of them are men, most from the south, and, as all Italians, they love cars, especially low, exotic ones that hug the road. Upon seeing them up ahead, I have often had to jam on the brakes of the Matra as they waved me over with their little red boards, the kind you see at school crosswalks. They try to look official and angry as they check your papers, but then they ask to look under the hood and drool at the engine. They smile sheepishly until you smile back with the bright idea to offer them a chance to drive. And with that gesture you are pals for life.

Past there you have to crawl through the towns of Pienza and San Quirico but with a concerted effort you can make the whole trip in less than half an hour, including a few minutes to get over the shakes.

~

Candace was with me that day so I took it slow, and, not having to concentrate, went off the road just twice.

We met sultry Silvia, who represented the owners, in Montalcino's central *piazza*, in a bar. It's a wonderful little spot, original Liberty style like the old cafés of Rome and Paris, in a cozy *piazza* in the center of town at an elevation of

1800 ft. It is hemmed in by buildings all around, even on the east side, where three tall arches once framed a magnificent view of the distant Apennines. I say once because some modern bird-brained visionary walled up the view to create storage space.

So we sat at an outdoor table and Silvia drew from her briefcase a beautifully organized folder of her houses.

We weren't used to such professionalism in Italy. We had grown accustomed to agents who doubled as butchers, pizza men, or funeral directors, all of whom used as reference material odd bits of paper kept under floor mats or in old sandwich wrappers. But that wasn't all. Silvia pulled out another folder of glossy photos in plastic sheets. This was a major improvement over no photos at all, or ones that looked as if they had been kept on the dashboard since the war.

We were speechless when she announced that the house in the magazine was one of *thirteen* equally beautiful for sale. We gazed at abandoned abbeys, magnificent sprawling wheat mills, a small church with an adjoining monastery, and even a large-arched *fornace* where not long ago the locals fired their roof tiles and bricks with wood. With the judicial investigation keeping all money safely in mattresses, we had the pick of them to ourselves. I had always bypassed Montalcino, for while we adored its wine—Brunello—the land we had seen was either one dull dry valley or another, dark and narrow with no views. But Silvia assured me that her houses were in a zone we'd missed: over five thousand acres of rolling hills owned by Banfi, the biggest vintner in

Montalcino. I was hesitant to ask, but Silvia read my mind and said, "Would you like to see them all?" I loved Silvia. She looked enticing in the third seat of the Matra with her raven hair.

"Did you know that Mormons are polygamous?" I inquired.

Candace smiled, dug her nails into me and said, "Let's not talk religion, dear."

~

A few miles south of town the pavement ended and we turned onto a dirt road and began a slight descent. Everything seemed to change all at once. Until then we'd passed only leafless oaks, but now they gave way to lush, broad-leafed evergreens, *corbezzolo* with its leathery leaves and red, cherry-sized fruit, *lentaggine* with somewhat finer foliage and clusters of tiny flowers, and tall ilexes of the holly family. On the banks were broom, sage, and pink and white wild roses with centers as yellow as the sun, and on the dry slopes there was pampas grass and wild laurel. The air was misty and warm, as only spring can be. We had crossed from the cold interior into the warmth of the Mediterranean Sea. The sunlight grew hazy.

Yet I wasn't truly impressed until we came over a crest. A vast valley sprawled before us—knolls, gullies, and sharp bluffs—heaving like the ocean. My eyes traveled to a river below mountains, behind which shone a patch of the Tyrrhenian Sea. And there, in the sea, rose the Isle of Elba, where Napoleon had been exiled. Scattered in the valley, lakes glittered in the sun, and nestled on the hills were castles, towers, and ruins. All for sale.

"Who has been hiding this place?" Candace murmured.

~

We wound down the mountain past a tiny hamlet and roller-coastered onward through the hills, some bright green with wheat and crowned with a few trees, others covered in vines, still others dark with woods. In the quarter of an hour since we had left town there had been, in all that space, not a soul in sight.

Beyond a long row of cypresses that ended at a graveyard wall we came to a stop outside the hilltop village of Camigliano. To the south, the hill dropped in a wild slope, and to the north the country rolled full of olive groves. We continued on foot past an old castle into a *piazza*. In a hundred steps, we had walked through the town. Broad stairs rose to a Romanesque church and a narrow alley beyond. Down a long flight of steps, under an arch filled with the fragrance of wine cellars, we came into a *piazzetta* with a covered well. A handful of narrow houses stood side by side, some giant cacti bloomed with pink flowers, a big red cat slept in a sunny window, and above it hung the cage of a drowsy blackbird. *"Buongiorno, come stai?"* the bird asked politely, then, without awaiting a reply, drooped and dozed off again. The only other sound was of a wooden ladle being tapped against a pot.

Camigliano ended in a sharp bluff. Silvia pointed across the gulch to a house alone on a perfect little hill, with open country all around and the Amiata volcano looming in the distance. "That is the first one," she said. "It's called Centine."

Although it had seemed a stone's throw from where we stood, it took ten minutes by car to wind our way there. The house had long, panoramic views, except the one of Camigliano, which was too close for comfort. And while the exposure yielded unimpeded vistas, it also offered no protection from wind and sun. But its walls were beautiful. They were, in Tuscan terms, "new," built in 1890 by a fine mason. The stones were all cut, the corners shaped, and the joints so tight that there was almost no need for mortar.

"Sign the check," I whispered to Candace.

"Calm down, Chum," she whispered. "We have twelve more to go."

The next jaw-dropper was called Belreguardo. The derivation was obvious: the view could stop your heart. The house had a walled-in barnyard and a picture-perfect arch. However, on the dirt road alongside, Banfi's tractors and trucks flew by as if the drivers were getting paid per cloud of dust.

We drove to Lavatrice, with rambling outbuildings popping up like mushrooms. But it was for sale with only two acres of land, which were completely surrounded by

Banfi's vineyards, so we would be escaping the frying pan by jumping into the fire.

In Tuscany, the lack of land available with old *poderi* is always a problem. In the 1960s the houses were abandoned when the *contadini*, who for centuries lived in them and worked the surrounding land, moved to cities for factory jobs. The new owners saw little value in the dilapidated houses, but the land around them was considered pure gold. The first thing they did was to cut down all the trees so they could plant right up to the walls. When, twenty five years later, there came a demand for these ruins to be restored as country homes, the land-owners grudgingly included an acre or two without which any house would be hard to sell. Those wanting only a weekend place were glad to have the land around them worked by others, for it guaranteed an expense-free and well-manicured view, but this was a problem for a budding farmer like myself.

After tours of the first eight houses, we were enamored but confused. Thankfully, Silvia suggested lunch. We trailed meekly after her, trying to sort out what we had seen—which house had what features, what land went with which view—but we managed only to churn muddled images.

"Which did you like the best so far?" Silvia asked.

"The condo in Miami," Candace said.

The wine reprieved us. It's amazing how something that in excess can turn you into a babbling idiot can, after one glass, give you a razor-sharp mind. Everything made sense, most of all the steaming plates before us.

We were under Banfi Castle in a little place called Il Maruchetto. We had let Silvia do the ordering so we could concentrate on her folder and didn't realize until the plates arrived that we were in one of the best seafood trattorias in Tuscany. The sea is less than twenty miles away, so the owners, who were from the Amalfi coast, could easily satisfy their dedication to serve the freshest fish. The first course was clams, mussels, octopus, prawns, and squid steamed in white wine and garlic. Then came spaghetti with mixed seafood in a piquant tomato sauce, followed by a plate of *fritture*: squid, prawns, and tiny fish fried in a light batter, crisp and tender in your mouth. The chicory, steamed and then dressed with olive oil and balsamic vinegar, was just the right thing to balance out the *fritture*. We washed all this down with a Banfi Pinot Grigio—one of the rare white wines in this region. Profiteroles followed and that arterial cement, *tiramisù*. We were drinking our espressos when the owner shuffled over with complimentary grappa in glasses the size of birdbaths. As we talked, the grappa fog thickened.

"Would you like to see the other houses?" Silvia asked.

"Why not," Candace said.

"What houses?" I slurred politely.

"I forget," Candace said. "But let's follow her, and see."

~

The next two ruins remain a blur to this day. There was either a mill on a hill (or was that Don Quixote) or a castle on an island (or was that The Count of Monte Cristo), or the other way around. The third was a good-sized church attached to a small house, doors ajar, windows gone, weeds and broom out of control. When Silvia went to find the best way in, Candace announced that she had to pee. Urgently. So did I.

We beat a path through the scrub toward the back where Silvia wouldn't see, but just as we turned the corner a leprechaun of at least seventy popped up before us. He had a Swiss farmer's cap askew on his brow, a hoe raised above his head, and a tidy little vineyard right behind him. He smiled, then, with surprising force, brought his big hoe down.

"Buongiorno," he chimed.

We chimed back and held our bladders.

We chatted about the abandoned place, the view, and the well-kept vineyard that he had worked these many years that was now all for sale.

His eyes grew mischievous. He leaned on his hoe and grinned a happy smile. "I bet you won't guess in a thousand years who I am."

"I hope a urologist," Candace said. "Because I'll need one in a minute."

"What did she say?" the little man asked, because she'd said it in English.

I told him she couldn't guess and neither could I.

"Oh, try," he coaxed, and leaned harder on his hoe.

"For Christ's sake," Candace pleaded. "Try anything. Say the Easter Bunny."

I guessed he was the local wine expert. He laughed but I could see his disappointment. "Do I dress like a wine expert? Now honestly."

"Oh my God, I'm dying! Get me a priest," Candace, pleaded.

"*Un prete*, a priest," I said.

"That's right!" the little man roared. "How the devil did you know?"

"Your eyes," I said. "Is there a place to pee?"

We passed up buying the church. Since it was from the tenth century, it was a national treasure that could not be touched; only the small house could be restored. The sun was low; the billowing clouds started pinking in the sky. We drove down a hill, through a creek, then up a winding path, and as we bumped along, Silvia said, "Now you'll see the jewel in Banfi's crown. It's called Il Colombaio."

We passed a farmhouse where a family was returning from the vineyards with their hoes, then down a steep hill into the forest gloom and over a stone bridge.

"From Roman times," Silvia said. "When the Romans still knew something."

A quarter mile later, the road wedged so tight between two houses, I was sure we'd lose our mirrors. The homes were beautifully rebuilt, with lush gardens and a vineyard sprawling behind.

"A high rent district?" I asked Silvia.

"That's Soldera," she said. "He makes the best Brunello in all of Montalcino. Sells for $200 a bottle in New

York, so he can afford to plant a daisy now and then."

We swung around a little graveyard and a church with an odd onion-shaped steeple full of bells. Wisteria climbed up the walls and flowerpots lined the steps. A large old man with a slight limp carried a rabbit in his hands. Smiling, he waved the rabbit at us as we passed. Beyond the church, the road, so little used that grass grew in its middle, wound toward a house in the distance.

"That's the last house on the road," Silvia said. "Beyond it is a canyon."

We turned off onto an overgrown trail; wild roses scraped the bottom of the car.

Silvia stopped. "From here we go on foot."

We climbed up a rise with no house to be seen, for we were hemmed in on both sides by a most eerie sight. It must have been an olive grove long ago because we could see fresh olive shoots reach out from brambles hopelessly entwined. Uphill, in a dryer spot, we could see enormous, ancient olive trunks just half a foot high—the rest had been cut, with each stump sprouting dozens of thin new saplings. Below the hill the land flattened out, covered by weeds. Suddenly Candace veered off the path, ran to the thickest patch, reached in and pulled out a shoot with two feeble grape leaves. She held it up triumphantly like Salome brandishing St. John's head. "Here it is Chum," she laughed. "Your very own vineyard."

The Hoer.

41

6 ~ THE JEWEL
IN THE CROWN

I was like a five-year-old on Christmas morning. I started counting the rows of fallen vines but they were so covered in brambles I gave up and ran to the woods. Two hundred feet above the house, past a pasture, was a dense forest. Where the canopy of trees blocked the sky, the smaller trees had died and formed an impenetrable web.

"Chum!" Candace hollered from below. "Chum!"

The women had bushwhacked their way another hundred feet and now stood at the house. On its north side was an odd-shaped structure with tall, crumbling stairs and a low stone shed. Candace was under an open part of it, half her body immersed in an outdoor *forno*—a big brick oven— that had baked Tuscans their bread through the centuries.

"It's in perfect shape," she yelled. I knew then that this was our house because she had always wanted an old *forno* as much as I had wanted a vineyard. From the outside the oven was a block of stone, eight feet square, with a terracotta roof and brick chimney. Its opening was at waist height, arched and just large enough to slip in a small pig. I stuck my head in. Inside was a miracle of architecture, a perfect dome, more shallow than Brunelleschi's in Florence but built by the same method: tapering rows of bricks. You could heat it up in a couple of hours with bundles of twigs, then brush aside the ashes and put in leavened bread, a chicken, ribs and perhaps some sausages. Then, toward the end, bake a tray of tarts, and sit and eat until the sun went down.

We hacked our way with sticks around the house. Its west face soared above us like a fortress, with varying roofs, its tower against the sky, and arches yawning darkly in the fading light. To the south was the courtyard. Around it, the house rose two stories high on three sides, but on the fourth a short wall had buckled to the ground. A fig tree had taken it over, its twisting, entwining branches reaching from wall to wall as if to guard the place. Working my way on all fours to a sagging arch, I crawled inside.

I felt I'd entered a fairytale my grandmother told me long ago. The walls were massive, three feet thick, dank odors drifted in the air, and silence reigned. In the cavernous gloom loomed vaulted ceilings, moldy walls, and arches. Through a narrow opening, a stairway twisted into the dark. Nooks and niches were cut into the walls, and there were broken chairs and a wooden table with one leg crumbled, like a stricken beast on one knee. And hanging from the wood beams overhead, rows and rows of darling little bats.

Upstairs, in a voluminous kitchen, was an open hearth and a low brick structure with two holes in its top for iron pots where sauces had stewed for hours. The beams, runners, and brick tiles of its once-whitewashed ceiling were now black with soot, and where the rain had come in through broken tiles the walls were streaked with its stains. Wood doors stood ajar, askew on their hinges. In one room, there gaped a hole in the floor where salt, dripping from hams hung from the beams, had eaten away the mortar.

Ancient books and papers were heaped in a corner: an old mildewed copy of Chekhov's *Three Sisters*, curled postcards, books of prayer, and, tied with a coarse string, a sheaf of letters written in magnificent handwriting between the years 1791 and 1822.

Except for the hole in the floor, the house seemed sound; there were no caved-in roofs or crumbling walls, so a wide-eyed dreamer could easily fool himself into thinking that the house needed only a few roof tiles, a coat of paint, and a broom.

I must have been first in line when they handed out wide eyes.

~

I wanted to walk the property that Silvia said stretched almost a mile beyond the hill, but the sun was low and the woods too dark to begin wandering. So we searched nearby and found a creek in a hand-laid stone bed below the house.

It was sunset. The clouds had softened along the lower sky. Layers of hills, with mist between them, reached the horizon. Cypresses stood darkened, and a dove cooed in a tree as if saying farewell to the light. The sun fell behind the clouds and the sky began to burn. Bright shafts burst out with flaming edges and far to the south rain covered the hills with a drifting dust of gold. Then the mist in the valley and the lower sky turned red, and the sun sank out of the clouds and touched a mountaintop.

"Chum," Candace whispered. "God built this ruin for you."

7 ~ STEP ONE:
HOW TO POUR

It's one thing to find the ruin of your dreams, but it's quite another to pay for it. All our money was in our house; if we sold it we could buy Il Colombaio and perhaps do the renovations, but until it was finished we'd have to camp out in a tent. We knew that a thorough rebuilding could take up to two years—six months for the permits and the rest for digging, scraping, plastering, chiseling, hand-wringing, and crying—and if for all that time we had to rent, it would break us. I had a new book out chugging along fine but who knew when it might come to a stop, and renovations always cost much more than one expects.

Depressed by all this, I was awoken from my snooze one warm afternoon by Candace yelling, "Anna, Anna!"

I thought that Anna, whoever she was, must have just arrived, but Candace came and sat beside me and recounted a story. Anna had a fine house with lush gardens near Monte San Savino, but she lived deep in the woods. Being in her late

50s and alone, as much as she loved her place, she wanted to be near people. So she sold. But the house she bought in town had to be restored ground to roof. Needing a place to live, she sold her new house, this time with an innovative feature: a live-in gardener: herself. The Germans who bought her house only wanted it for some weekends and their annual vacation, so as long as it was available then—and lovingly cared for the rest of the time—they were as happy as clams, as was Anna.

We decided to sell our house *alla Anna*. The ideal buyers would be ones who lived far away—like Pluto—so they would seldom come, but since we knew no Plutonians, we looked to the next most distant place: Canada. And even better than just any old quiet, would-never-intrude Canadian, we found a buyer to whose heart we could appeal: Candace's rich investment-banker brother, engulfed by his job seven days a week, *six thousand miles away.*

No sooner did we decide to move than we contracted the famous Tuscan disease: The Doubts. La Marinaia was home. Plus Candace had the studio in town, and Buster loved his schoolmates and his schoolmates loved him back, especially Benedetta, a mischievous, dark-eyed, seven-year-old beauty, who seemed to have mistaken Buster for a pony and was always on top of him, showering him with kisses. Then, of course, there was the greatest tie of all: the Paoluccis.

So we decided not to decide. The only way to make sure we didn't jump into something was to get off the continent. We'd go sailing for the summer in the northern reaches of British Columbia to do research for my historical adventure novel, *Ghost Sea*. We packed books on Tuscan architecture, grape growing, and winemaking.

Just before leaving, we took a leap toward real winemaking: We bought ten demijohns—a bathtub-full—of young wine. We knew from our reading and many visits to wineries that just-fermented wine takes on magical qualities if placed for a year or two in new French oak barrels. From the oak, the wine extracts tannins, which not only give it a long life but also make it more complex. One also gets the delicate vanilla flavor from "toasting"—setting aflame and scorching—the insides of the barrels. There are complex interactions between the once-live wood and the still-very-much-alive wine, like micro-oxygenation, and other terms I never understood, which bring out unprecedented softness, roundness, and flavors. In other words: the harsh, abrasive vehemence of youth is made mellow and wonderful with age—like us.

So, along with the wine, we bought two new oak *barriques,* barrels, which hold two-hundred and twenty-eight liters each. Why that bizarre measure is used irks me just as much as why there are 5,280 feet to a mile. We bought the *barriques* from our local Consorzio Agrario, which, for lovers of country stores, is like dying and going to heaven. They have beehives, rootstock for vines, tiny oak trees inoculated with truffles, tools of incomprehensible purpose, humane weasel traps, traps for zapping bugs, stainless steel olive oil vats, poles and wires for vineyards, and live chicks, ducklings, and piglets.

We went to the Consòrzio in Paolucci's three-wheeler Ape, which is best described as a mechanized vest—it's so tiny you don't really enter it as much as you put it on. It has a small truck-like flatbed in the back and a motorcycle engine with a cylindrical capacity of 50 cubic centimeters, which, in cookie-baking terms, is a quarter of a cup. It goes uphill roaring like a lion at the pace of a snail. So between loading, gossiping, stopping at Crociani's to taste his just-bottled Vino Nobile, unloading, then stopping at Bazzotti's for a bite of sausage, then again ten feet further to help Scaccini grab his runaway goat, delivering the two barrels *one mile as the crow flies* took us from morning until night, but sitting in the dim light of our underground cellar, the sight of those two superb oak barrels was enough to wet your eyes.

Then we had to transfer the wine from the demijohns into the wood. This is child's play if you have a pump, but we didn't. What we had was a small funnel from our kitchen. A fifty-liter demijohn of wine is over a hundred pounds. Fortunately, it has two large handles for lifting, so we gathered our thoughts, lifted, tilted, and poured. One of the great miracles of physics is the way wine pours from a demijohn: first nothing comes, then a giant glug, then nothing, then another glug, resulting in wine cascading down the barrel and the walls. This does have two advantages: it takes that fussy, new sheen off the barrel, giving it a veteran look, and it lightens the demijohn for the next attempt.

Once we learned to control the glugs, we watched in amazement as the wine poured evenly, swirled in the funnel, then suddenly filled up, and gushed right down its side.

At this point, we reverted to the technological brilliance of my youth when I managed, with a four-foot hose, to suck the last drop of gas out of my father's car.

Siphoning is simple: in the case of wine, you wrap yourself around the demijohn, grab both its woven ears, lift, and place it on a stool. Give the hernia a little rest, then place the barrel near it on the floor. Insert one end of a clear tube into the demijohn, and put the other end in your mouth. Suck until your cheeks, lungs, and other organs implode. Then, sit and wonder why God chose this very day to turn off gravity, because through the tube you saw the wine rise, but, for some *Madonna puttana* reason, the wine would not flow down.

Next, your loved one suggests raising the demijohn end of the hose a smidgen because it might have sucked the bottom. You respond with sarcastic laughter but do it when she's not looking, reinsert hose in mouth, suck with super human strength, and watch the wine shoot up the hose and out your ears and nose.

From here on it gets tricky.

8 ~ A NEW FRIEND

*O*nce in a lucky while, you meet someone and know at first glance that you'll be friends for life. Before we left to sail in the Pacific, we went to meet Tomasso Bucci. He's known to his friends as Tommi, the director of Banfi's high-tech winery who also had the final say on the sale of the thirteen *poderi*. When Candace and I entered his office he sprang to his feet, walked his slight but athletic body around his desk, and shook our hands with the kind of warm and profound look reserved for dear friends.

"I heard you're a writer," he said.

I told him I do have a try at it now and then, and he laughed.

"Ah, but you have the books to show for it. I'm a poet but all I have are sheets of paper in a drawer."

After a half hour of friendly chatter, he unrolled a military map of the area that identified every building in the valley. Then he brought out the twin of the impressive folder we'd seen before. We went through it together photo by photo, house by house, accompanied by his unsolicited narrative and surprisingly candid assessment. While he seemed quietly proud of each one, pointing out particular merits, he never hesitated to point out the flaws. Then we came to the jewel in the crown: Il Colombaio.

His eyes smiled and he sighed. "If I were a rich writer, Ferenc . . . It's such a poetic house, and with seventy acres, two hills, a canyon, and some of the best land for vineyards in Tuscany. The ancient Romans had some of their finest vineyards there." Then he looked out through the window at the long, vibrant green of the Tuscan landscape, and said with the sincerity and wistfulness of a child, "that's not just a piece of land. It's a tiny kingdom."

He took us for a walk through the Banfi winery, from its giant stainless steel tanks and cellars filled with the mesmerizing fragrance of oak and wine to the tasting room with a view over the vineyards. As we were tasting what seemed like our hundredth glass of wine, in walked a jovial, rotund man in his sixties. We were introduced to Banfi's CEO, Cavaliere Rivella, "Cavaliere" being an Italian knighthood, which he received for his life's achievements among which was, literally, creating Banfi. I had heard of Rivella; he was notorious for attracting film starlets with his genteel manners, lusty gaze, and impeccable taste in wine. He was also a Marxist. Now this acclaimed Marxist, with his cravat and deep smile, walked up to Candace, gazed into her eyes, and, without a hint of ostentation, bowed, took her hand, and raised it to his lips.

He talked about Il Colombaio, about the perfect ten acres to the southwest of the house ideal for planting Sangiovese—the grape used in Brunello—and about the clay to the west where he'd plant Merlot, while Cabernet would thrive in the gravelly fields surrounded by woods farther up. Then he became excited as he said, "you know, to the south, I found some walled terraces, which I'm sure were built by Etruscans. *O Dio,* the Romans would never bother with so small a piece. It's a perfect funnel for the afternoon breeze from the sea. If you could rebuild those terraces, maybe six of them, and plant, I don't know, maybe an acre," and he swallowed, "of Syrah. Terraces on a hill looking at the sun. My God, what a wine."

He emptied his glass, and like Lawrence Olivier after a wrenching soliloquy, moved with sure and measured steps offstage, into the twilight.

~

We walked back through lush gardens with Tommi to his office.

"Not to pry into your decisions," Candace said, with surprising clarity for someone who had just consumed her body weight in wine, "but if the fields of Colombaio are so perfect, why haven't you planted vines in them?"

"I wish we could," Tommi replied. "But look. " He

went to the map. "This is the property." Bordered in green pencil was a bizarre shape that looked like a sitting rabbit, with paws, long ears, and a saggy butt. Within the boundaries, and shaded in red, were six patches of various shapes and sizes. "The patches are the fields where you can plant vines. The rest is *bosco*, woods, that cannot be touched. Except for the ten acres below the house, they're all small fields. You have to plant carefully and maintain them with small, specialized machinery. We have vast vineyards with lots of space at the ends of rows for big machines to maneuver. How could we expect a tractor operator, who all his life drives like a cowboy, to think for a few hours a month like a brain surgeon?" Then he lowered his voice and looked us straight in the eye. "A place as magnificent and unique as that—certainly the nicest I have seen in southern Tuscany—should not be wasted on a big corporation. She needs someone to love her, like a writer, or a painter." Then he stopped, laughed, and pulled out the lining of his empty pocket. "Or a poet."

We drove the long and twisting back roads home in silence through the dusk. I sat alone in the arbor and watched the lights come on, one by one, in our magical town. I thought about Il Colombaio. It seemed to have been created for someone who would treat its eccentric woods, fields, and vineyards with respect. It needed someone who'd be thrilled by the daily joys of tilling a long-abandoned field, planting rootstocks in the cold spring earth, and watching the miracle as they would sprout and green and send forth clusters of grapes. It needed someone to nurture its small vineyards, which, in turn, could produce fine grapes for generations. Seductive wines could come out of the cellar and stir emotions that a profoundly sensuous wine can: laughter, romance, and dreams.

9 ~ MR. GLUE

We spent that summer living on our sailboat in the northern reaches of the mountain-bound British Columbian coast. We sailed among misty, desolate islands and forests where the Kwakiutl nation once thrived, where ice-capped mountains and deep inlets still guard the coast from encroaching civilization. Their abandoned villages with fallen burial poles and decaying dugout canoes are as mysterious and intriguing as any place on earth. For over eight thousand years they lived off the sea, sharing the bounty, beauty, and mystery. They conquered no neighbors, nor did they pile great stone monuments. They lived a simple life in which everyone was cared for.

Anchored at night under the stars, alone among the silent islands, we ate fish, crabs, clams, and oysters we harvested ourselves, and I felt a sense of fulfillment the Kwakiutl must have felt. And in that empty, peaceful place it struck me that the Etruscans had lived in their hills in much the same way. They, too, were satisfied with the rewards, both sensory and emotional, that a simple life can bring. And they seemed to have instilled it into future generations because even the younger Tuscans have the same contentment with their modest lives today.

~

We came back in September ready to take the leap, hoping and praying that Il Colombaio had found no other lover. But I was worried by Tommi's welcome. He was courteous, said he was happy to see us, but he seemed distressed. He tried his best to make small talk but without enthusiasm. Finally he couldn't hold it in any longer and told us that Centine—the house of our second choice—had been sold, and so had four other of the beautiful ruins. He looked away and fell silent. After a pause, he added in the most circumlocutory and delicate Tuscan fashion that Il Colombaio, the small kingdom, had for weeks been in *trattative*, negotiations, with a wealthy industrialist who produced most of the world's adhesives. A preliminary agreement had been signed, and he was to fly in the next day to iron out some details regarding the rights to Brunello and to sign the contract. Tommi looked so shaken I thought he might cry.

I sat there, as stunned as a jilted lover. I had lost out to a guy who made things sticky. I lost out to Mr. Glue.

~

I just had to go see her one last time. We drove up to where the path began, Buster trotting happily, with a stick for a sword challenging the army of brambles. Candace held my arm to console me, and I looked everywhere but at the house and tower up ahead. Well before the house, we turned onto a trail wide enough for carts that lead through the woods to the top of the property.

This time there seemed a sadness to the forest. The path was damp and the air full of autumn scents. Ahead, the woods opened into a field of giant oaks, and among them the Mediterranean scrub was once again taking hold. Beyond the field was a view over the valley, below us was the odd-shaped steeple, and in the distance lay the hamlet of Tavernelle. The evening mist rolled in.

Buster's battle cry cut through the air from up ahead.

"Mom! Dad! Come look!"

"Not now, dear," Mom said.

"But Mom, you won't believe this."

"Angel, please be quiet. Mommy and Daddy are plotting how to kill Mr. Glue."

But Buster is not a child you can ignore. He doesn't often demand attention, but when he does you had better give it, or he'll come and take it out of you in spades. This time, however, he fell silent and waited until we caught up with him. He had struck a curious pose. He was standing facing us in a shallow ditch beside the road.

"Okay, what is it?" Candace asked.

"Oh, nothing. Go on with your plotting," the little brat said.

"Tell me or I'll choke you," Candace said.

Instead of speaking, he raised his little stick and like a magician made a circle in the air, stepped aside, then pointed to where he had been standing at a dark blob on the ground.

"Jesus Mary," Candace said. "I think I'm gonna die." Right there, by the side of the trail, where anyone could have found it days ago, squatted a *porcino* as big as the Brat's head.

"Lord love you," Candace said and hugged him so hard she almost crushed him. But the Brat had just started. He dashed ahead, stopped in a ditch, crossed his arms and whistled. There behind him was another big *porcino*.

"Get me some smelling salts," Candace said. Buster ran ahead, stopped, whistled, *porcino*. Then he went and did it again.

Candace cut the stems with her nail file to leave the mycelium in the ground so it could sprout again next fall.

"They'll be picked by Mr. Glue," I grumbled.

"No, dear," Candace corrected. "Dead men don't pick mushrooms."

She had no idea what true words she'd spoken, for that very night Mr. Glue would be, at least figuratively, dead. The Marxist and the Poet made very sure of that.

~

In Italy, *calcio*—the glorious game of soccer—is considered more sacred than the Pope's hem. Children live by it, husbands leave wives for it, and the makers of Viagra get rich from its effect on fans of the team that loses. A normal weekend game can set a neighborhood on fire, a championship can cause national mourning, and an international match can overturn the ruling government (which has happened 43 times since the Second World War). This is precisely the same number of times the Azzurri—the national squad—has had its butt kicked at home. Some say there's no connection, but they're the same skeptics who say there is no Easter Bunny.

That night the national squad was on the ropes. They were behind 2-0 in a vital match they had to win to move on toward the World Cup. A deadly hush had fallen on Italy. At halftime, millions of prayers were whispered, offering sacrifices, bribes, pleas, and even the renunciation of tomato sauce for a day.

Then the phone rang. It was Tommi Bucci. He spoke so fast that it took me some time to figure out he wasn't talking about the game. He was talking about Il Colombaio. At a cordial meeting with Rivella—the gentlemen's gentleman—Mr. Glue became arrogant and pushy. Rivella had turned beet red, sent a hand signal to Tommi calling him over, written two words on a piece of paper, and pushed it toward him.

It said, "get Máté."

10 ~ *THE BAPTISM*

In most countries, real estate deals are concluded with agents, a written agreement, and a checkbook. With Bucci and Rivella, there were only four glasses and a bottle of champagne. We were in a room high in the castle, overlooking the Banfi estate: the lake below us, the hills dotted in ruins, and the wooded mountains. We had a few laughs and a couple of toasts, then Tommi reached into his pocket, rattled around, and pulled out a ring of keys and handed them to me.

"To your house," Rivella said, raising his glass. "And may it be reborn, starting tomorrow."

I was taken aback. I wanted them to know that I kept their needs in mind. "I should give you a deposit," I offered. "Or an insurance policy, or something written in blood?"

Rivella smiled but instead of a verbal reply, he gave a slight swipe of his hand as if shooing away a gnat.

The deal was done.

Tommi thought we should have blueprints of Il Colombaio to take home with us that night, to dream over and to help us redesign the inside of the house, so we followed him in a more or less straight line back to his office. My hands trembled as he gave me the plans.

"You know," Tommi said. "I rebuilt our family house in Abruzzi. It took me a year, but it was the best year of my life."

Then the phone rang. *"Ah, buongiorno, signore,"* he said. From his expression and gesticulations we knew it was Mr. Glue. We heard Mr. Glue raging clear across the room. He raged about the access road he wanted Banfi to build for him, about the payment schedule, the transfer of Brunello rights a year earlier than discussed, and about an option to buy the house next door if he ever so decided. Tommi let him rage. Occasionally he said, "ah, ha," or "oh, yes," then paused to let Mr. Glue wind himself into a frenzy again. Finally, he interjected with utmost calm. "But all this is somewhat irrelevant, Signore," he said, "because Il Colombaio was sold to a writer this morning."

Mr. Glue fell silent. For all I know, he's still there hanging on the line.

We had to rush from Tommi's office to pick up Buster from the Sacred Heart of Saint Agnese, the convent that looked down from the walled town onto our house. There, watched over by nuns, he spent most of his days drawing, playing and running from Benedetta.

Dinner was a challenge with blueprints on the table. We pored over them, reorganizing rooms, demolishing partitions in the stables, sketching a stairway to the tower, and pondering how to lay out the kitchen in the pigsty and where, and in which direction, we would plant our vines. We planned our first meal there, for that coming Sunday. I didn't sleep that night. I didn't even bother closing my eyes.

Eating Sunday lunch out was, by then, a family tradition. During my house-hunting journeys, I would ask locals for the best restaurant in town, not the fanciest or most expensive, but where the chef—almost always the owner—cooked straight from heart.

One sure way to make an Italian fall in love with you is to ask his advice on food. Whether it's which cheese to buy at the market, or which is the best fruit stand, or the name of his favorite restaurant, his eyes will light up, he'll take a deep breath, and he'll begin a detailed and passionate oratory.

Armed with local knowledge, not only of the best place to eat but also the best dishes to be had there, we've had the most remarkable meals of our lives. I remember the roast suckling pig at Latte di Luna in Pienza; the white truffles with *tagliatelle* at La Torre in Monte Oliveto Magiore; the hare sauce at Da Mario in Buonconvento; the fried *porcini* at La Tagliola near Arcidosso; and of course the roast pheasant at Trattoria Sciame in Montalcino.

But this Sunday, after a morning of cleaning up our very own ruin, we would make lunch in the courtyard of Il Colombaio. We loaded our tiny Volkswagen Polo, a station wagon the size of a golf cart, with rakes, brooms, shovels, pruning shears, a sickle, and a wicker basket of food, and set out. It seemed an eternity before we arrived.

The autumn sun beat down as we stopped by the small, family-owned winery at the entrance of the dirt road that lead to our house to buy a bottle of local wine for the occasion. A middle-aged man, squat and solid as a mountain, greeted us with a big grin at his cellar door. When we told him we were the new owners of Il Colombaio and wanted to celebrate our first meal there with his wine, his eyes welled up. "I was born there," he said. And when I tried to pay him for a bottle of 1987 Brunello, he seemed hurt. "A gift to my old house," he said.

It's difficult to single out the emotion I felt as I stepped onto our very own seventy acres of Tuscany. There was joy and fear, calm and worry, anticipation and apprehension. The brambles now seemed twice as thick, the vineyard more dead than before, and the house, which in the twilight had been an enchanted castle, now in the light of day looked more like a heap of stone. The only solution was to stop emoting and dive into the work.

We threw out the old feeders and rusted farm gear from the courtyard, swept its paving stones, and dragged out the wounded table and made it a new stump leg. Candace and I stacked bricks and stones from the tumbled wall to make a good place for the fire and sent Buster off to gather firewood while we set up the double grill to roast ribs, sausage, and pigeon.

Ten minutes later Candace yelled after him to bring the firewood right away or she'd add him to the meal.

"Coming!" he replied, and we heard his footsteps thudding down the hill. He swung into the courtyard with two measly twigs in one hand and the other hidden behind his back. As Candace was about to wring his neck, he whipped his hand into sight, and said "for you," and handed her a bouquet of lovely, dark *porcini*.

~

We had learned from Nonna that when you roast meat in a double grill that stands vertically beside the fire—instead of burning and charring right over the coals—you must allow at least an hour and a half to slowly cook it properly, turning it every quarter hour. Cooking it right means a tasty crust forms over the ribs; the sausages lose their fat and become dark mummies full of flavor; and the pigeon skin crisps like parchment, each bite a bit of heaven.

Most people in our situation would have enjoyed the rest of the morning running their eyes over their sublime friary—the ancient stones, the graceful arches—but not I. I had the vineyard to liberate from its tomb. I bid my family good-bye and dove into the brambles. I cut with the shears, beat with the shovel, ripped with the rake, and slashed with the sickle. After an hour of pouring sweat, there seemed to be more brambles than before. Candace brought me a glass of wine, waited until I drank some, and then suggested an alternative tool: a bulldozer. I glared at her.

In the end, after a two-day battle, I managed to clean up exactly four distorted, half-dead vines. Since there was another half-acre to go, I calculated that to finish what remained would take the rest of my natural life. It was then that I revealed to Candace my brilliant idea: a bulldozer.

~

Our first meal at Il Colombaio was a wonder. With the warm wind bringing the smell of roast ribs, *porcini*, and pigeon, and my heart full of failure, I ambled back to our ruin, where the courtyard was bursting with colors, smoke, and voices. The crippled table was now covered with a yellow tablecloth, the wine bottles glowed, the dishes gleamed, and in a tin were twigs of rosemary and flowers. The grilling rack was packed with browning bits of meat.

Buster was born not only to eat but also to help his mom in the kitchen. After masterfully chopping basil to sprinkle onto tomatoes and mozzarella, he put his skill to slicing up a big white bulb I hadn't seen before. "Fennel, Daddy," the little chef beamed. "Mom found it in the garden."

It's amazing how a bite of roast meat and a generous glass of hearty Brunello can restore your energy, how the second glass will have you laughing with all your heart, and how the third will leave you looking around for a secluded place to ravish your wife. We uttered a stream of can-you-believes: can you believe that twisted beam, the shape of that cornerstone, the curve of the well, that old tile, the clear sky. Then Candace had enough. "Buster," she gave the order, "go up the road and find some *porcini* for the Paoluccis." She grabbed me by the hand and we went through the old kitchen and up a rickety ladder into the tower.

"Close the door," she said. She kneeled on the pile of old letters and pulled her blouse over her head.

"There is no door," I said.

"Then pull up the ladder, crank up the draw-bridge, just for God's sake hurry up."

~

We'd had our first meal there, hacked the brambles, made love, drunk wine; Il Colombaio had been baptized. And was ours forever.

11 ~ THE LAST CONTADINI

*N*ow came the moment we'd been dreading: telling the Paoluccis.

I dropped off the *porcini* on the way home that night and escaped quickly, saying Buster was asleep in the car. That was only a half lie. He was lying down; the fact that Candace was sitting on him threatening him not to make a sound is neither here nor there.

For the next few days, we managed to avoid them. If we did see them working around the house, we stopped, but only for a short chat. By Thursday, I noticed tension growing between us, and it occurred to me that maybe someone's loud mouth had already spread the news. I silently concocted a dozen stories for why, in a year or so, we would move out of a house we loved, and worse, move away from our dear neighbors—our family.

"We have to tell them, tonight," I said to Candace.

"I'll make a Tarte Tatin and we'll take it over," she said.

"I'll draw a picture of the cows," Buster added.

The three of us walked in silence up the moonlit path, past the vineyard that had started all the trouble. Atop the hill, the town was full of shadows, with a few lonely lights scattered among the houses, and the steeples loomed dark and somber in the moonlight. The frogs seemed to croak sadly in the pond. The only cheery thing was the smell of the baked apples.

The Paoluccis were all in the kitchen at their usual evening places. Nonna sat on a low bench inside the huge fireplace knitting a shawl, Rosanna was at the table sewing buttons, and Carla was helping Eleanora with homework, rolling her eyes and nudging her when she lost concentration, and Paolucci was on the other bench, carving a new wooden handle for a knife. But while their places were the habitual, the mood was downhearted.

"Get some wine, Rosa," Paolucci commanded.

Rosanna went to the cellar and brought back a magnum. We put the pie on the table. Tuscans never thank you for things you give them; neither do they expect thanks when they give things in return. Only Eleanora uttered *"Che bello,"* and snuck a bit of crust.

We ate and drank but the joviality was missing. We had finished the tart and made a good dent in the wine when Rosanna broke the lull in the conversation. "We heard some news about the house," she said.

We sat still.

"We knew it would happen sooner or later," Paolucci

added. "I'm surprised it hadn't happened before."

"Things change," Nonna said. "But as long as we have our health."

"I'm so sorry," Candace blurted. "We should have mentioned it before." She seemed near tears.

"You've heard?" Paolucci said. He looked utterly surprised.

"Heard what?" I said.

"Must have been Piccardi," Nonna sighed. "His mouth is bigger than a cow's."

"No one asked him to keep it a secret," Paolucci chided. "Besides, it's his job to transfer the house."

I tried to follow. "You've *heard?*"

"Heard what?" Paolucci said.

"About our house?" I said.

"*Your* house!?" he exclaimed. "I'm talking about *our* house."

"*Your* house?" I gasped.

"Are you drunk?" Paolucci asked. "Of course *our* house. *This* house. The owner wants it back. We have to move."

~

The Paoluccis' news was a bigger shock than I thought ours would be. We had always assumed that the house and land were theirs. We knew they had been there for almost forty years, planted the vineyards, the olives, the cypresses and pines which now all but covered the house. The girls were born there, his father had died there. All the other neighbors owned their lands and houses; why would we have thought the Paoluccis any different?

In fact, the Paoluccis were one of Tuscany's last *contadini*, a modern version of medieval serfs. For hundreds of years, most of the land belonged to either the church or big landowners. One famous estate in Val D'Orcia, near Pienza, had 600 people working and living on it. The estates were virtually independent duchies with their own churches, priests, courts and law, jails and even their own judges. Who wrote the laws is a fair question. Most of Tuscany's old stone houses, the *poderi*, housed an extended family of the *contadini* and the animals they cared for. The houses, land, animals, machinery, even the seeds were all the landlord's property; the *contadini* owned only the clothes on their backs, but they had use of the house from birth until death. In return for working the land allotted them, they received one-half of all they produced: in grain, olive oil, wine, piglets, chickens, and eggs. This was called *mezzadria*, or crop-sharing system.

After The Second World War the state put an end to this. Most of the landowners had to offer the houses and some land around them for sale, at a reasonable price, to the *contadini*. Many bought. The Paoluccis didn't. The new laws would have permitted them to stay on until death, but that would have meant having an unpleasant relationship with the owner. However, the law called for compensation if they were asked to leave, so at least they wouldn't go with empty pockets.

"So where are you going to live?" Candace asked, panicked.

"Near my sister in San Quirico," Paolucci said. "Two towns west of here."

"We're moving that way, too!" Candace cried. "Three towns west: Montalcino."

"We're forced out like you," I lied through my teeth. "Her brother owns half the house and it's his turn to use it for the next five years."

Candace almost choked on her tart.

"That's great," Paolucci said, jumping up. "Then we'll still be neighbors! Rosa, bring more wine."

"There, I told you," Nonna said. "Things change. But as long as we have our friends."

And with her weathered, knobby hand, she wiped away a tear.

12 ~ THE NEW CONTADINO

*T*o become a farmer in Italy, you have to do more than just dig dirt. To qualify for subsidies and tax abatements, you must officially become an *"imprenditore agricolo,"* which involves passing grueling trials of physical and mental endurance. You begin by standing in line for endless hours in order to receive reams of documents: pamphlets, books, and legal declarations. Next, you read for endless hours the reams of documents written millennia ago by a twisted Latin scribe who was paid by the ton. Then you stand in line a hundred more times to obtain various permits and applications because you have learned—to your amazement—that your farm is not merely a farm but an infinite cosmos of diverse subphylums such as forests, olive groves, vineyards, pastures, seedable fields, unseedable fields, soil, subsoil, nightsoil, ground, underground, ground water, surface water, flora, fauna, birdlife, wildlife, nightlife, good-life, archaeological patrimony, artistic patrimony, and post-trauma alimony, all of which are overseen by individual ministries and departments—multiplied by three levels of government: municipal, provincial and federal—all of whose offices are strategically and equidistantly dispersed (to insure survival of the bureaucracy in case of nuclear attack) all over Italy, with no recognizable exterior signs and not an available parking space for miles, whose office hours are determined by a game of darts each morning, offices to which "you'll have to come back next week or next month," because the office is just moving, or has just moved and left no forwarding address, or because the bureaucrat responsible is at lunch or in a meeting or in a stupor or dead.

And then you have to pass a written test.

The good news is that it's a modest exam of only twenty questions. The bad news is that the twenty questions are chosen from a monstrous volume containing 2,679 bits of farming-related information, a half a page long each.

Since Italian law does not differentiate between say vintners and duck farmers, this single test must cover all imaginable aspects of farming. Hence you will be required to commit to memory such diverse and remarkable tidbits as the average gestation of a sow; the first sign of a testicular hernia in a bull; the specific gravity of freshly excreted cow dung (to avoid overloading a cart); the mating habits of wasps, ticks, and mites; when sap runs, when it doesn't run, or when it just jogs in place; how to recognize seventeen types of wheat, six types of corn, and the color of a mature chestnut; and the most crucial piece of knowledge of all—which end of an earthworm is the tail, and which the head.

This would be a daunting task even in your mother tongue, but when you try it in your *fourth* language whose first sentence you uttered at the age of forty-five, then you'd be forgiven if you lose the vivacity of your smile. Admittedly, my Italian had improved drastically since its first deadly days, one of which I waltzed into our local butcher's, looked at his hanging, homemade salamis, smiled knowingly, and in order to impress him not just with my Italian but also my dietetic awareness, asked, *"Mette preservativi sulla sua salsiccia?"*

His face went red. I had no idea why until Candace whispered, "You just asked him if he puts condoms on his sausage."

By then the butcher recovered and said, utterly composed, "That, dear Signore, depends on what you have in mind."

So I dove into the chapter on how to remove a stuck egg from a chicken.

~

I studied for months. I memorized everything. You could shake me from the deepest sleep and I could recall, without blinking, the zodiac sign of any given weasel. I was ready.

The examination is given only twice a year, so one is well-advised not to fail; otherwise, during the next six months, one will get wiped out by the burden of a 20 percent sales tax on everything from tractors to land. To retain what I had learned, I mumbled the correct answers day and night, and one day in town I walked right past Piccardi. He grabbed my shoulder and blurted, "Wide awake! It's morning!"

I begged his pardon, explaining my obsession with studying for the exam. Piccardi rolled his eyes in disbelief. "You memorized all that? Why? You crazy?" And he rustled furiously inside his briefcase, pulled out a crumpled sheet, and shoved it in front of me. On it I saw the words *Esame per Imprenditore Agricolo,* and below it the twenty questions.

"Here," he chided. "All you need to know. They have been the same twenty questions for more than thirty years." Then as I stood there crushed and speechless he walked away but called back, "Italy, Ferenc. Remember? Italy!"

~

After all that struggle I almost missed the test.

I had known there was a deadline for filing applications, but as always I left it until the last minute. I sauntered into the Ufficio Agricola Imprenditore Novelle, just outside Siena, on Saturday—the deadline day—at 11:30, forty-seven minutes before official closing time. At the entrance I was almost bowled over by a hefty Tuscan farmwife, cursing and striding out at great speed, who then leapt into her three-wheeler and roared up toward town. I was alone in the office with a great oddity: a charming bureaucrat. He examined my documents, complimented me for filling them out right, then handed them back to me and, smiling, said goodbye.

"But the application," I pleaded, "You have to keep my application."

"Delivering it by hand is against the law," he chimed. "It has to arrive by mail with a postmark of today."

"But the post office," I pleaded, "It's in the middle of town and closes in twenty minutes."

"Eighteen," he corrected.

I almost bowled him over as I headed for the door, cursing and striding at great speed. The post office was only three miles away but the problem was Siena—a walled town closed to traffic. I floored the Matra. It screamed uphill toward a town gate and the only parking lot I knew of. So far so good, except the post office was nearly across town. I parked, then ran along the ramparts looking across the valley at Piazza del Campo—the view, a Michelin one-star; turned sharp left into the Piazza of the Duomo, the Cathedral with its richly decorated thirteenth Century façade—three stars; below the green-and-white-striped marble walls—two stars; down the curving marble steps, under a dark, dank, stinky archway—no stars; along a narrow ramp with a view of the Basilica of St. Dominico—ho hum; up the main *corso* with some beautiful *palazzi* and into the square where the post office sat, and where the distraught farmwife on her three-wheeler roared up the steps, jumped out, and ran in before me. Two minutes to go. In a wonderfully controlled and sub-servient manner, she explained to a gruff man behind the grill that her family's future depended on a stamp for her envelope and a postmark with today's date on it. The gruff man got the stamp, ran it across a wet sponge, and even stuck it on for her, but the postmark, he explained, was impossible. It would

77

be applied by workers in the back, but not until Monday since it was now one minute to closing and everyone had left. The farmwife smiled so widely it chilled my blood. Then she reached below the grill and grabbed the gruff man's arm. "If I leave without that postmark, your arm is coming with me."

The gruff man froze. Then, with his free hand, brought out a rubber stamp. And you have never seen a more beautifully articulated postmark in your life.

I was next. I pushed in my envelope, took a deep breath, and with my heart in my throat, murmured, "Same problem. Same stamp. Same...." And I stared full of meaning at his arm.

~

The exam was in a frescoed room in Montepulciano. There were about thirty of us; I recognized a few—the pharmacist, a doctor, a hairdresser, the undertaker, the loan officer from the bank, and the chief of police—all of whom, because of tax write-offs, were suddenly budding farmers. The exams were handed out, the clock strictly observed. A terse older gentlemen with a mustache and wire glasses barked, "Now begin," and added menacingly, "and not a word of talking." Then he sat behind his desk and watched us like a hawk.

Italians take things literally. No one talked. But the terse man never mentioned yelling. Within minutes the room was abuzz: "Hey Luigi, what's the right word for rot?" And "Oh, Albertino, how many nipples on a cow?"

I was first to hand in my paper. The terse gentleman looked it over, put it down and said. "Well done, Signor Máté. One last question on a topic I heard interests you: *Mette preservativi sulla sua salsiccia?*"

13 ~ NO TURNING BACK

*T*o rebuild an ancient ruin in Tuscany, where every brick and stone is part of a protected, historical monument, requires patience, passion, perseverance, and four times your body weight in official documents: permits, affidavits, plans, authorizations, applications, and supplications.

The only way to survive this is to hire Piccardi, the human bulldozer. Piccardi is sophisticated, middle-aged, and tall, with a voice that makes a hurricane sound like a whimper. He is what's called here a *geometra*, something between a junior-level structural engineer and an architect. I believe this position unique to Italy, where, after the Second World War, some bribe-riddled, shoddy construction led to many a new building suddenly falling down. While a *geometra*'s real task is making sure stacks of documents don't topple, Piccardi's greatest asset lies far beyond the basics: it is his unique skill to accelerate the normally interminable bureaucratic process. With a few chosen words, he can bring the nastiest, most intransigent and often vindictive paper-pusher to tears. I witnessed some of his verbal slayings, and although I have yet to learn the entire narrative, I got the gist from key phrases such as: "your sister," "a trampoline," "a trained pig," "cement," and "a painfully long old age spent in abject poverty."

So Piccardi did the social work, Candace drew the plans, and I took the job of Designated Worrier. If the last seems like a trifling occupation, try to imagine a colossal puzzle of unfamiliar pieces, e.g., a crumbling stone ruin, the solving of which requires five stonemasons and an eighty-foot crane, costing you a *barca di soldi*, a boatload of money, per day. Plus materials, plus tax. The fact that you can get drunk at lunch and laugh about it through the afternoon does not diminish the nervous sweat trickling down your sides.

The only thing that restored my faith in this absurd, heartbreaking shortcut to the poorhouse was the arrival of Pignattai. He was in his early fifties, short and tough—he used to be a mason—and as highly strung as a tuned violin. Moreover, he had the aesthetic instincts of an artist. Pignattai was *il capo*, the chief, of the masons. He owned a small construction firm: eight workers including his brother and himself. His job was administrative; he was in charge of planning, purchasing, and fretting. In a terse three-minute speech he could solve the dozen problems you'd lost sleep over for days, a structural dilemma was overcome with a quick and perfect formula written with his finger in the sand, and he could place the best beam in the right spot before you could point and say "There!" Plus, his workers showed up day-in and day-out—a miracle in Tuscany.

Piccardi, Pignattai, and I sat together one afternoon to discuss the whole project. Piccardi quibbled to get a firm financial commitment, the best overall estimate. Pignattai argued for the most leeway in construction. Overwhelmed by it all, I excused myself halfway through for a refill of grappa. When I returned they were both silent. A page full of numbers was pushed before me. On one side was written the annual budget of a small African nation, and on the other was scribbled 35,000 lira (approximately $25) per hour.

Piccardi wanted to stick with Africa, but I could see that Pignattai wasn't happy. "I can do it by contract," he said, "I'll be on budget and the house will look fine. Or," he paused and looked me in the eye, "we can do it together by the hour. You've built a boat and a house before, so you can do the woodwork and we'll do the rest. That requires much faith on your part, for you have to trust that we will do our best. But that way we can make changes as we go, as we learn. And with the *bellissime* shapes the house already has, we can create a museum piece."

How could I resist?

Piccardi didn't even look up. He knew. He scribbled something on a piece of paper, folded it, and stuck it in my shirt pocket.

"What's this?" I asked.

"The address of the poorhouse," he said.

Pignattai took a long breath and for the first time smiled. "I'll never get rich this way," he said, "but at least we'll have a good time." He asked Piccardi when the restoration permits would be ready. Piccardi guessed optimistically about six months.

"So when should we begin?" Pignattai asked.

"Monday," Piccardi said.

"Fine," Pignattai said. "We'll call it cleaning and maintenance."

On Monday morning, in drove an eighty-foot crane.

"In case somebody asks, we're checking the gutters," Pignattai said.

We walked carefully through the house. I pointed out to him how solid and sound the place seemed, all it needed was a bit of paint here, a touch of plaster there, some rewiring, and of course new plumbing. The only sign of the latter was a closet-sized affair on the second floor that hung out over the courtyard on two beams, like an outhouse lifting off for Mars. In its center was a ceramic hole with two notches for your feet. A pipe hung unceremoniously from it.

I showed Pignattai the few beams I thought needed a little reinforcement, the tiles to be replaced, and window frames in need of glue, and as a writer I expected him to note all this on his pad. But the pad was blank.

"How will you remember?"

"It's all up here," Pignattai said. And he tapped his head.

~

We had to go to Mantova for a few days. Candace was invited to show her paintings in the Casa di Rigoletto, perhaps the most beautiful small *palazzo* in the entire city.

Mantova is magical. Surrounded by three lakes, it was once heavily marshed, hence the city was at one point as reliant on canals as Venice. The canals are long gone but *piazze, palazzi*, and churches remain. Although most people consider the works of Mantegna, Pisanello, and Giulio Romano to be Mantova's main treasures, for me its most remarkable contribution to world culture is *raviolini con zucca—ravioli* with squash. If this seems sacrilegious, try it with a bit of melted butter on top and you'll soon change your mind. The *ravioli* is small and hand-made. The pasta is so thin it melts in your mouth, releasing a burst of orange squash. This dish goes perfectly with a nice Soave or Valpolicella, and primes you for the main course: to put it crudely, mule stew. Believe it or not, this is a sophisticated dish served in fine restaurants as far west as Verona. It's unforgettable in both presentation and aroma, even though it tends to have the specific gravity of lead. But, oh, what flavors and how well it goes with a bottle of Amarone.

~

A few days later, after a farewell lunch, we rushed through three hundred or so curves, tunnels and bridges between Bologna and Florence to catch a glimpse of Il Colombaio before sunset and to see if there was any noticeable change.

It was a thrill to meet the masons. Fosco, the oldest, was the head man. He was as stocky as a boxer with a nose that had been broken a few times. Piero, second in command, was tall, with bright, anxious eyes, and movements that seemed to go in all directions at once. Georgi was fat and sang constantly. The three of them together were a hundred and eighty six years old. Alessandro was young and quiet, and then there was Asea. Asea was from Nigeria. He had started studying architecture but decided he liked the outdoors better, so he signed up as a *manovale,* a mason's helper, or in this case four masons' helper. The masons depended on him as they would a mother. Lean but robust, he had a remarkably warm laughter, which burst out at the slightest provocation.

As we were finishing handshakes and introductions, we heard a rumble from inside, and then a loud, angry curse. It was Pignattai. Thinking he might have dropped his note pad, we went around to the courtyard and into the first of three low stables. Light came through the chinks around the door at the far end.

"Kind of bright in there," Candace said.

"It's the low sun," I said.

"There's no window in there. Plus the light's from above."

Women have strange notions.

We edged through the stables, stepping over piles of rubble I didn't remember seeing before. An unease shot through me. I tried to push open the low wooden door that led into the last stable, above which was a room and above that the tower. The door opened an inch and then stuck.

"It is bright in there," Candace repeated.

"It's probably a work lamp," I said, and put my shoulder to the door. It gave. I was bathed in daylight pouring from above, because above there was no longer a ceiling, not over the stable, nor over the room above it, nor over the tower above that. The floors, ceilings, and roof were gone. We stood beneath four tall walls and sky. Candace let out a little yelp.

"Pretty cool," Buster said.

"Buonasera," Pignattai said. "We've started."

14 ~ THE WINE STAR NEXT DOOR

Angelo Gaja has laser eyes; I'm pretty sure in an emergency he can use them to weld steel. He also makes some of the world's very best wines. It was he who started the wine revolution in Italy back in the early seventies by insisting on superb quality—quantity be damned. Within a few years, *Wine Spectator* called his Sori Tildin "the finest Italian red ever made," and wine critics gave his Sori San Lorenzo an amazing 100 points. His better wines currently sell for $400 a bottle. He is charming, articulate in a handful of languages, obsessed with quality, amusing, and completely mad.

I was swinging my adze one afternoon, removing the rotted surface of a giant oak beam, while the masons were hammering away furiously, as they were wont to do after the bottles of wine they consumed at lunch, when a racy red Audi came up the drive, its bottom banging on the road's raised center. Out leapt a middle-aged man with a surprising bounce in his step as he came toward the house. He stopped and talked to Asea, who pointed at me and called out, "Dottore!"

I had become Dottore the moment they learned I had a university degree and the name stuck except in emergencies, which at the house arose every twenty minutes. These were punctuated by Fosco's frustrated cry, "Máté!" with endless E's trailing at the end. Upon the shout, all came to a halt and everyone waited for me to announce some architectural or engineering decision.

In an instant the man stood before me. His right hand shot out; his left held a wooden box used for expensive wines. "Sorry to disturb," he said. "I just came by to make your acquaintance. We're neighbors. I bought the wine estate next door to you today. I'm Angelo Gaja."

At first the name didn't click, but I was thrilled to have such friendly—if somewhat high-strung—new *vicino*. Then he handed me the box, upon which was branded his famous name.

"Madonna," I exclaimed. "Gaja of the great wines? I've read your biography."

He dismissed it with a smile and began a deluge of compliments about the house, its shapes, the view, and the romantic woods. I in turn, praised the vineyards he'd just bought, the medieval wine cellar, and the seventh-century (now deconsecrated) church called Santa Restituta with its fanciful, onion steeple. How beautiful it looked from our house. On parting, we seemed to have been friends for years.

Until his visit, I had quite forgotten about planting the vineyard, not from caprice, but simply because I was deluged with work on Il Colombaio. I had to drive from our old house every morning six days a week, those two hundred and forty grueling curves each way, and by the time I arrived, the masons had not only been banging and wrecking for an hour, but seemed to have set records inventing new problems for the day. Piccardi took care of the bureaucracy, but the decisions of the renovation—locating the openings, excavating the urine-soaked dirt in the stables, building the new internal stairs, three bathrooms, the furnace, drains—were all left up to me. The family did come on Saturdays to eat lunch on the crippled table in the courtyard, and Candace, with her painter's eye, helped with big decisions; however, small matters such as whether to frame the opening in old brick or stone, sizes, shapes, angles of window sills, door sills, steps, chimneys, and roof overhangs all fell on my shoulders.

I was also the carpenter of the house. I adzed, chiseled, and knifed away the rot of the old usable beams, reshaped old runners, and hand-planed new ones so—once stained—they would blend in with the old. In spare moments, when "Mátééé!" wasn't ringing in the air, I became Asea's personal helper. I gingerly scraped and cleaned the mortar off old roof-tiles, chipped crud from bricks, scrubbed travertine pieces with a wire brush, and then hauled it all away and piled it safely to be used once the destruction ended and construction began. So the vineyards were on hold, until the weekend we had dinner in a twelfth-century villa in Arezzo.

Sandro Cecchi is a true Tuscan gentleman: handsome, charming, and so warm he melts women's makeup at ten paces. He's versed in art and literature but also a fine boar hunter, traveled but not ostentatious. He loves to laugh, eat well, and drink excellent wines. He lives with his companion of many years, Joyce, in the four-story villa his family has owned for over six centuries. It's full of ancestral paintings, notebooks from explorations of his great-grandfathers and uncles, armor, fine furniture, and quiet elegance. He adores Candace, enthralled by her abilities as painter, pilot, sailor, adventuress, and all-around siren.

Sandro invited us to dinner with a few of his friends. The dining room was full of candlelight and chatter. Fragrances drifted from the kitchen where Joyce's revered cook, Anna, bustled. After a *porcini* soup, we were on to our second course—an enormous Bistecca alla Fiorentina, a slab of steak, cooked rare, crusted in salt and sliced into mouth-watering pieces—when Sandro opened the wine Gaja had given me and poured. We swirled and sniffed it. The chatter died. We sloshed it around in our mouths. No one said a word. Even after I swallowed, the wine miraculously elicited brand new taste sensations.

During our year in Paris, we often saved up and bought a half bottle of expensive old Beaune or Meursault, but I'd never in my life had wine this good. The room remained still as everyone sipped again.

"What is this stuff?" Candace finally asked. "I never knew such complex flavors existed."

Her young dinner partner gave a mocking smile. "Sori San Lorenzo 1989, Signora. A national treasure from Angelo Gaja."

"Oh, him," Candace said. "The guy next door."

We explained that Gaja had bought the adjoining estate, and how he graciously brought the wine as a gift.

"Nice," Joyce said. "A $400 calling card."

They handed the bottle around the table as if it were the Holy Grail.

The room was now abuzz with the news that Gaja, from Piemonte, had bought into Tuscany. They speculated as to why and noted how fortunate we were to have such a brilliant neighbor who could teach us all about making an exceptional wine. I humbly informed them that, exhausted from two months of tearing the ruin apart, I'd never ever have the strength to raise a shovel, never mind plant a vineyard. As if on signal, the elegant dinner guests began their attack.

"Perhaps because you're from North America you don't understand this event," one said.

Then, one after another.

"You're crazy! You have to plant."

"You are in blessed company my friend."

"Gaja has been called the King of Italy."

"How did Italy ever let *you* in?"

"You should be extradited."

"Or exiled."

"Or executed," Candace suggested.

Sandro, a gracious host, tried to calm the mob.

"Ferenc, let's say you were a zealous Catholic," he began thoughtfully, "who enjoyed the church and its beliefs all your life. Then one day, unannounced, the Pope moved in next door. Would you thumb your nose at him and suddenly turn heathen?"

The mob murmured unveiled threats.

"Enough," Candace said rising to her feet, her face turning redder than the flowers on her Norma Kamali dress, bought years ago with her last pennies in Manhattan.

"Where are you going?" Joyce gasped.

"Where else?" Candace said. "To get my man a shovel."

15 ～ BURIED TREASURE

After two months of renovation, our house looked freshly bombed. Splintered beams leaned against it, torn-out window frames were stacked here and there, and bits of twisted metal were scattered everywhere. All that was left intact were towering walls, without floors or ceilings or roofs, reaching grey and forlorn to the sky. And even those massive walls—in places three feet thick—were, I was told by Fosco, riddled with holes, hollowed by the centuries and by animals that scurried in and out of them to nest, scooping out a bit of mortar with them every time.

Perhaps it's best to explain how these houses were made. The method of construction had not changed since the Etruscans. The first stones were placed directly onto hardpan, or sandstone or rock. The walls were built double-faced, without forms, using a string to keep a straight line, and a lead line to keep it plumb. Mortar, a mixture of sand and lime, was used between the stones. Between the inner and outer walls, the space was filled with mortar and rubble: bits of rock, broken bricks, whatever was around. When the walls reached the first floor, huge wood beams—oak if the owners were wealthy, chestnut in the mountains, poplar on the plains—were set into the wall about three feet apart. These supported the floors above. Set across these beams, at one foot intervals, were smaller beams, *correnti*, as thick as an arm. On these were laid *mezzane*, literally "halves" or half-thickness bricks. Atop these went a thick stratum of mortar and on top of that another layer of *mezzane*, for the walking surface of the floor above.

Still with me? I'll tell you the rest.

The roof, sloping thirty degrees for drainage, was made the same way as the floor up to the first *mezzane* layer. Then came a layer of *tegole*, massive slabs of terracotta a foot wide and nearly two feet long, with the sides turned up to form a kind of canal. Since water could get in through the seams between them, a layer of *coppe* was then laid over the seams. These were also made of terracotta, tapering half-pipes the same length as the *tegole* that overlapped each other to form the outermost layer of the roof.

Tuscan houses so constructed are virtually maintenance-free and last forever, as long as they are lived in. That is, so there's someone to notice the first leak in the roof caused by birds building nests under the *coppe* and cats robbing the nests by pushing the *coppe* aside. In such circumstances, you simply climb to the roof, reset the *coppe*, give the cat a kick in the ass, and your roof is set for another hundred years. The problems began in the 1960s when government programs and the bright lights of big cities persuaded many to drop the plow and pick up a time card, leaving the houses to the birds and cats.

With the walls weakened by weather and beast, the first step was to take a hammer and chisel and chip around each stone to get the seven-hundred-year-old mortar out. This was no small task, considering our house had about thirty thousand stones. But with patience, time, and an unlimited supply of wine, you *can* keep that mortar flying. At this point, I hired myself as the sixth mason, for nothing else could be done until the old mortar was replaced with much stronger modern cement.

We were chipping away one sunny afternoon after my five-course lunch at Trattoria Sciame and my *quarto* of wine, a shot of grappa, and an espresso, all of which turned me into a human missile. Chip, pound, chip, pound, whistle while you work. Fosco was to one side of me, Asea to the other. Little did we know the house was about to launch a swift counter attack. We had become engrossed in our work, speaking only rarely on two inexhaustible topics: sex and cars, and were reaching deeper into the wall, when all of a sudden my chisel hit something soft and squeaky.

They came like a cloud of locusts, like bees swarming from a hive, out of holes, cracks and joints between the stones, squealing, jumping, and running up our hands, up our arms and down our backs: a stampede of panic-stricken, oddly adorable mice.

That was the only day we all went home early.

~

From that moment on we took the precaution of flooding the walls with a garden hose to evict the tenants. A month later, all the outside stones had been chipped and cleaned, and exactly what held the walls together at that point, I don't know to this day. From dawn 'til dusk we poured cement from buckets into the tops of the walls, with what seemed like the Niagara Falls of Cement, and then we filled by hand every crack between the stones.

But what you don't want to see between the stones of a thirteenth-century house is twentieth-century dead-grey cement. So, while it was still soft, we scraped out the last half-inch of cement and scrubbed and brushed each stone so not a trace of cement was to be seen. Then we made *colored* mortar out of white cement and yellow sand and added dyes to recreate the tone of the yellowish earth that had previously held the stones. Finally we repointed each stone with the dyed mortar, then scrubbed away the excess until before us stood bombproof but ancient-looking walls.

From first chipping to last scrubbing took about three months. By then I was on the edge of an emotional, physical, and financial chasm. I talked of stones and dreamt of stones, and when I looked in the mirror I was surprised not to see a stone staring back. What saved me from going over the edge was the day I found the buried relic.

Remember, animals had lived on the ground level. Here the floors were covered with large paving stones. After removing them, we had to dig out a foot of urine-soaked dirt before we could build *vespaio*, or hornet nest: a raised, concrete sub-floor under which air could circulate to keep our new floors free of humidity. We dug out the dirt in the goat pen and pigsty, and then came the cows' stable. Fosco and Piero had just begun to lift stones when Piero gave a shrill cry that would have shaken the windows, had we any.

A big stone stood on edge, and below it showed the perfectly sound upper rim of a large, buried terracotta urn. I got down on my knees and started scraping with a wooden stick. At first I thought it was just a piece of rubble used to shim the stone, but the more I dug, the more urn came to light. It was painfully slow going but I was certain I had discovered a treasure. When I had dug inside it past my wrist, it began to get dark, and the masons grew bored and went home. I was glad they did; I didn't want them to set eyes on the gold.

I knew these urns. They had been in use since the time of the Etruscans as the principle means for storing everything from olive oil to grain. Judging from the size of the opening and shape of the urn's shoulders, I had a good arm's length to go. I dug. There was a small Etruscan ruin near us, so I fantasized of finding the treasures of a lost city like Troy, or if not Troy, Mycenae, with an urnfull of gold bracelets and necklaces, or even the golden mask of another Agamemnon.

Then I convinced myself that this was just the first of many urns, perhaps a lake of urns that helped hold up the house. It got dark. I needed light. I needed Asea's fire.

~

For lunch in Tuscany, a mason eats as well as any bank director. Each day at a ten to twelve, Asea would stack his beat-up wheelbarrow with shavings and cuttings from my beams to start a blaze. The masons all brought out their towers of stainless-steel pots—four little pots stacked upon each other and held together by a handle—each containing a different course of their four-course lunch. It began, as you might expect, with pasta, followed by a stew or slice of roast, heated on the coals, or sometimes a piece of veal or sausage grilled on the flames. Then salad or sautéed spinach, and finally, desert. All this was accompanied by a bottle of wine and hot espresso fresh from their personal espresso maker bubbling in the coals.

So I stumbled in the dark and found Asea's wheelbarrow. I groped about for wood, wheeled it back to the urn and set it all ablaze. The urn glowed in the light, and on the wall danced the shadow of a hunched grave robber.

I dug down a few more inches when I remembered the time. I hadn't phoned Candace and Buster to tell them I'd be late. I drove to Tavernelle, ran down the steps into the little dungeon that doubled as the bar and asked to use the phone. Vera growled and flicked the lever that measures phone time. Sometimes she didn't even growl. She never smiled, except once when—having heard that Candace was a painter—she asked her to appraise a small painting which her grandmother had left her, a painting that one neighbor thought was a genuine da Vinci. Which it turned out to be. Printed on genuine paper by a genuine machine, somewhere around the year 1985.

When I returned to dig, the moon was up, the fire down, and I still had a half an urn to go. I was losing faith. Why wasn't it full? Why bury a big empty urn instead of hiding a smaller one that would be harder to find? Unless they had to hurry. Before an attack—an invasion. In which everybody died. I was getting deeper, closer to finding the lost treasure of a whole nation, when I felt something with an edge. I scraped around it with my nails, careful not to do damage. I took a piece of burning wood in the wheelbarrow and held it flame-down. At the bottom of the urn was a clay box, the kind we use for jewelry, glazed beige and green, colors this region has used since time began. But in it were no jewels, not even a coin. There was just one letter wrapped in an oily cloth, which preserved it by soaking the paper through, but also made the ink run and very hard to read.

At home that night, holding it against the light, I could make out the year 1782. The writing was in an elegant, florid hand. It was by a woman, strange because this was a friary. What little I could read was a letter of common love—if there is such a thing—about longing and dreaming and looking over the valley for the dust kicked up by her loved one's horse. But the phrase that struck me, not for its originality but for its fearless question was, "Do you really love me, or just love dreaming of me?"

The urn stands in the corner, where it was found, to this day.

16 ~ THE LOST SPRING

*F*abrizio Moltard came bounding through the wreckage below the house. In his early thirties, he had an intense appetite for life, but greater still was his love for vines. He seemed to have memorized and assimilated everything ever written in English, Italian, or French about planting and maintaining a high-quality vineyard, growing the perfect grapes, and producing the very best possible wines in the world. He could deliver a lecture on sub-soils in Margaux, rootstocks in Burgundy, or the best thousand-year-old clones to be found near Naples. He had been the agronomist to Frescobaldi, one of Italy's foremost winemakers, and now worked for the best: Angelo Gaja. We had just finished repointing the walls and were well on our way to the poorhouse when Fabrizio arrived with the *coup de grâce.*

I was working in my makeshift carpenter's shop—a net tied to four poles for shade, and a workbench cobbled together from a door—when he came, introduced himself, and explained that he had been watching our progress and had to come and see. He spoke like an opera singer, never stopping for breath, with the bizarre result that I started holding mine. Just before I blacked out he froze. He stared at my feet as if transfixed and I was sure it was a snake—we have deadly vipers in Italy, although they're so lethargic you have to pick them up and slap them before they'll bite you—that I just closed my eyes and waited patiently to die.

Fabrizio is half French. He whispered *"charogne,"* which means dead meat, and I thought he was referring to me. Then he picked up a lump of clay, went to an old barrel full of water, and began to bathe the lump. He scrubbed and scrubbed and I thought his brain had died from oxygen deprivation until he turned back to me with a fossil. It was a spirally, curly seashell covered with knobs. Where we stood was over a thousand feet above sea level.

"Must have been some wave," I said.

He didn't laugh. He held it out to me and said, with the gravity of Hamlet contemplating Yorick's skull, *"Mon Dieu. Ici on peut faire le meilleur vin du monde."* Then he stared at me as if I wasn't quite worthy of owning this patch of dirt, or maybe even being alive.

The reason for his shock is that some of the world's greatest wines are from grapes grown in soil full of lime. He grabbed a nearby shovel and began to dig. A backhoe had cleared the area for my shop, and the soil had been turned and softened by its teeth. Fabrizio dug about a foot down in the rich soil and picked up an intact shell.

"You have good soil on top, full of minerals and microbiological colonies that will give good flavors to the grapes. Most people would thank God just for that. But you also have the slopes for good drainage, perfect exposure to the southwest, and the sea breeze in the afternoon to moderate the heat so your grapes won't cook like they do east and south of town. But besides all that you have a subsoil of fossils, lime, which can give your wines a whole other dimension. You are a fortunate man, my friend. You will make great wine." He was so moved he actually stopped for breath. Then he became adamant. "But you can't plant your vines like everyone else in Tuscany. That's old and barbaric and yields no result."

I assured him that I wouldn't plant like anyone because I wouldn't be planting even a single vine. My only ambition was to put a roof on my house before I died. He waved me away as if shooing a fly.

"Of course you're planting," he said. "I can see it in your eyes."

I tried to assure him that was just dust I had scraped from the beams, and that I was so worn out by the house that the only wine I cared about was the one to run down my throat later that day. But Fabrizio wasn't listening. He was walking away, fossils in hand, and turning back he yelled, "he'll be here tomorrow."

"Who?"

"The soil engineer. To analyze the soil."

Then he was gone. Our vineyard had begun; the dream

was coming true. Yet every now and then—and I don't mean to sound ungrateful—I wish that fossil *had* been a viper coiled there at my feet.

Fabrizio grabbed hold of my life the way a tornado sucks up dust. He stopped by every day and spewed out future plans so fast and without a single question that the whole performance seemed a mere formality.

We walked the property. The ten acres in front of the house he called a no-brainer: Sangiovese, the grape used in Brunello. But he thought it not only dull but foolish to force Sangiovese into soil less than ideal for it. So we ran around digging holes like moles with Fabrizio on his hands and knees eyeing the hole and crumbling soil to check its structure and how it would drain. Then he walked back toward the house staring at the ground, stopped, and jammed in the spade. "From here south there's too much clay for Sangiovese. It would make a harsh, coarse wine. Here we'll plant Merlot. It will be exceptional. Petrus would give its left *coglione* for a piece of land like this." Then we started up the hill through the forest. There was a small field a half-mile from the house partly shaded by some oaks. Fabrizio surveyed it and gave an impish grin. "Cabernet," he announced. "But not Franc, you wouldn't like it. It tastes like hay; we're not cows. Sauvignon."

That settled that. There were two fields near the top, nearly five hundred vertical feet higher than the house. The small one faced southwest, and the other, a near-perfect amphitheater, faced south.

Fabrizio was breathless. "Feel that breeze from the sea. It'll come every afternoon when the heat rises inland. What cooling. What a perfect gentle maturation and just look at this soil. Good soil mixed with *galestro*: finely broken shale. Packed with minerals, and minerals mean flavor. Sangiovese here. You'll make a Brunello that will make a grown man cry. Maybe we'll blend it with the Campo Casa, Field of the House, and, maybe we'll keep them apart. With this difference in elevation and soil, they'll be totally different wines; they might make the perfect blend."

As we walked the west tip of the bowl, he looked worried. "This is pure *galestro*. Too demanding for Sangiovese. Plant more Cabernet; it'll grow anywhere."

My head was reeling. I never thought we'd be planting various vines because Montalcino is known for Brunello, so why stick our necks out growing Cabernet and Merlot?

"Would you plant water lilies in the desert?" Fabrizio asked. Case closed.

We sat on the front steps looking at the soil reports.

"We have a wide variety of soils," he said, "but they are at depth, so we have to force the roots and go deep to get those flavors. Most people here plant fifteen hundred vines per acre. We're going to plant three thousand. Competition will force the roots deep."

I protested about twice the costs to plant, twice the amount of work to prune and tie, but Fabrizio gave me one of his "why are you alive?" sighs and went on.

"True, you'll do twice the work, but the quality will be more than twice as good. There's only one problem. We'll need lots of water."

In our part of Tuscany, cactus grows wild. This is bad news for young vines, which—like the doomed tomatoes of Siena—might just curl up and die. In southern Tuscany during summer the rivers are dry, the creeks dust, the waterfalls hot stones. The only place where water is found with any reliability is in the grocery store. Springs were everywhere in the time of the Etruscans, as attested to by the number of stone fountains we found cut into hillsides, but that was long ago. Cacti grow in them now. Digging wells was not an option, for we'd heard from neighbors that most holes had come dry. But, as my dear pal Ruṣin put it, "Máté, you step into shit and it somehow comes out gold." Or, more precisely, we found the Fattois.

They were our neighbors at the end of the road whom we'd rarely seen simply because we never passed their house, until one day a young man with a large German Shepherd came loping from the direction of their barn.

"*Buongiorno,*" he yelled from a long way off. "*Sono* Lamberto Fattoi. *Che bel lavoro state facendo qui!*" He stared with doubt at the roofless walls.

Lamberto was in his late twenties and unusually calm and congenial, with a laugh so deep it enveloped you. This was the first of what would be daily visits. He'd spend an hour away from his own vineyards and olives to see our day's work, but mostly just to chat. Whenever my worries piled up, or my frustrations overflowed, Lamberto's visit would set things straight again.

I told him about the problem of the water, and he nodded. They themselves had to dig a lake, line it with clay, and dig ditches across the fields to capture runoff from the rains. But then his face lit up. "Francesco," he said—I had stopped forcing the locals to pronounce Ferenc and taken up the Italian version—"my dad hunts. He knows every inch of everyone's land. I remember him saying there was once a spring at Il Colombaio. I'll ask."

The next day, Ofelio, the elder Fattoi came, with a quicker step and a louder voice than his son. He said there had been a spring but it was now so overgrown he hadn't been able to get to it in years, but if I liked we could try and find it. Armed with sharpened machetes, we dove into the woods. Scrambling along wild boar paths—low tunnels in the dense scrub—sometimes on all fours, we hacked with our blades and crushed with our feet. An hour later, we stopped atop a slope. Sunlight trickled through the growth above.

"It's here somewhere," he said, sweating and bleeding from scratches. "Wait here," he said and dove into the gloom. There were crashing sounds then a loud curse. "Come, Francesco. Come!"

I crawled to the end of the tunnel and stopped just before a low bluff. Down below sat Ofelio, with patches of sunlight around him. At his feet was a big stone cistern and shooting into it was a stream of crystal water. Ofelio drank. *"Buono,"* he said. I drank too. Nothing in the world tastes more refreshing than water from your own spring.

Ofelio cupped his hands and counted as they filled. "Three liters a minute," he announced. "Not bad after a long dry summer, eh Franci?" And he beamed as happily as if the spring were his. "This is a blessing you know. It's the best spring in the valley." Then he poked his finger toward the sky. "He must like you."

17 ~ DANTE'S BEAMS

"*M*átééé!" Fosco's cry floated through the early morning mist. I found him standing before the pile of beams that had once held up the roof and floors of Il Colombaio. He held a pocketknife, waited until I got closer, and then like Jack the Ripper, began driving it full force into the beams. Once in a while the tip stopped with a thud, but much more often it sank down to the handle. "Rotten, Máté," he snapped. "Too rotten even to burn. We'll have to bury them." And, perhaps out of habit, or to make a point, he crossed himself.

The walls were done, but we had no roof and, as the morning mist attested, winter was on its way. We needed beams.

This is a bigger problem than it may seem. Sure, one could buy new chestnut beams from sawyers on the volcano, but even though they had been cut last winter they're not yet *stagionati*, seasoned, meaning they would dry and shrink no more. Beams of any girth take years before they're truly *stagionati.* And once under a roof, the drying becomes too fast and the beams crack, shrink, and leave nasty gaps at their bases in the walls.

This was the story I used to convince one and all. The honest truth was I did not want new beams, for the simple fact that they looked absolutely new. For centuries, the beams were made by removing the bark with a small draw-knife—a blade with two handles—a method that left all knobby imperfections. Instead, the new beams were cut perfectly square by an enormous saw. If I had wanted square, I would have used cement. I had seen ancient oak beams in chapels and *palazzi* and, there was no denying, I was hopelessly in love.

This may seem like navel-gazing to those accustomed to grid-patterned cities and a countryside divided into straight-lined fields, but in Tuscany—where all lines curve; where roads and boundaries follow the flow of the land, the gullies, the creeks; where roads are diverted to leave a tree; where in towns streets snake and house walls bend—straight lines look offensive.

Fosco, of course, was hoping for new beams. This was not due to a lack of aesthetic sensibility—I was to learn with time that he had more than I—but simply because he wanted the best for me: to save me as much money as possible finishing the work. The big expense would come in after the beams were set. There would be dozens of *correnti*, runners, to fit onto each beam. To achieve level floors and a well-draining roof above, these had to be on the same plane, child's play with a nice square beam, but a horror if you have to plane or shim both ends of every piece. However, I had an argument for that too. Laying *correnti* on irregular old beams might be real slow going, but then the whole house had been built slowly—stone by stone, by hand. And even though it had been changed and added on to over seven hundred years, the add-ons all fit together harmoniously just as the hills fit the countryside. I felt a deep obligation to have our labor blend with that of twenty generations. In the end, the choice was simple: did I want someone seven hundred years from now to look at a twisted, gnarled beam and say, "what a heart-felt piece of art," or did I want them to look at a square beam and sigh, "what a jerk."

So the challenge was to find old beams. But how? Masons doing other restorations threw out only the rotten ones; sound ancient beams were still holding up houses. I drove around to every renovation site in our part of Tuscany, pleading and begging the masons to sell me what oak beams they could. Most of them apologized but could not help, finally one of them said the owner could care less whether his beams were old or new, so he sold me a couple of gnarled beauties.

Two down, thirty to go.

One day Candace and I crossed Italy's central valley and headed east into the mountains of Umbria. There we hit the mother lode. Near the town of Monterchi—home of Piero della Francesca's Madonna del Parto, the pregnant Virgin Mary, with her earthly beauty and unearthly serenity—I ran into a mason who had just sold a house full of oak beams to a man called Dante, who planned to cut them into lumber to make old-style furniture. Dante lived farther east still, so east we went, nearly to the Adriatic Sea.

Dante was lean, terse, and quick to anger, but I liked his frankness. "Ah, a writer," he said. "I have the beams for you. What lengths do you need?"

I had made a list room by room and Dante, as articulate as any architect, explained to me exactly how much girth a beam of a certain length should have for optimum aesthetic effect. Less would look flimsy; more would look obscene. We walked through a muddy lot toward the back.

"I could sell you these," he said. "But they're fir and straight and about as dull as life. You want something more romantic, I can see it in your eyes."

I swore then and there that I'd wear sunglasses day and night; my eyes had given me away one too many times.

We stood at a pile of discarded beams dumped like pick-up sticks, too uneven and knotted even to cut as lumber; a heap of the weirdest, most twisted oak I had seen. I was in love and began to pull the pile apart. But it was lunchtime.

"Where is there a good place to eat," Candace asked.

"At my house," Dante snapped. "I'll call the wife so she can add more pasta," was his formal invitation.

Dante's wife was the largest suffering saint in history. But her looks were just the beginning; she could also lament, endlessly. Her duck sauce on *tagliatelle* followed by deep-fried chunks of rabbit were excellent, but at what a price. She lamented about the butcher, her sons, chickens, her youth, her old age and about Dante, who chewed, silent and nervous, often rolling his eyes. Only when she lamented about Italy did he finally cut in.

"There's only one thing wrong with Italy," he cried. "The Italians. Every one of them up against the wall." And, in case I missed the point, he machine-gunned the company. This from the man whose namesake was the father of the language.

Dante drove up to Il Colombaio two days later with a truck full of beams. The masons couldn't believe their eyes. They unloaded them, one by one with the crane, in silence. When one of my favorites hit the ground, I ran up and asked Fosco to come and have a look. It was a medium sized oak beam, somewhat squared off but by hand so all the adz marks showed.

"What do you think?" I asked, enthusiastic.

"Perfect, for the fireplace," he said.

"Above it?" I suggested.

"In it!" he snapped, and marched away—like a bull—to lunch.

Fosco did not eat with the other masons. He would stop

work a few minutes before twelve, change shoes, remove his shirt, wash down in cold water, don a fresh shirt and drive to a restaurant. It was always the same place, Trattoria Sciame in Montalcino near the Fortress, freshly remodeled with impeccable taste; a family-owned, little place with eight linen-covered tables. The mother cooked, the daughter served, and the father hung around, having taken care of growing all the chickens, vegetables, and rabbits for the restaurant. Fosco would take his daily table there with two other sworn bachelors from town, one the banker, the other the cobbler.

He would have his five-course lunch with wine, espresso, and grappa, then in a more jovial mood return to Il Colombaio, having spent the exorbitant sum of $8.00. As do most restaurants in Italy, Trattoria Sciame has two prices. I paid $19.50 my first time. The second time, with Fosco's introduction, I, as a regular, paid $8.00.

Tourists shouldn't take this as an insult, for this is how Italian restaurants survive. Regulars keep them afloat in low season, regulars who would never come if they had to pay full price. For a year, I became a regular, which had other advantages besides the price: not only would you get the best table—I needed it to draw the plans for the afternoon's work—and Mamma's special *dolce* that she made only for "family," but they gave you the freshest and the best of everything. When you asked if they had your favorite Guinea hen cooked in wine, she replied in code, "we do and we don't," then you knew that it was to be shunned, for it had been made the day before.

The special price most often excludes a receipt; in other words, the money goes undeclared, so the owner pays no tax. This is less risky than one would guess. One day I went to another of my favorite places, where I was also a regular. As I came in, two tables had been pushed together and were occupied by a half-dozen uniformed Guardia di Finanza, in the middle of a long and costly feast. These are the men who'll stop you on the street and fine you $1,000 if you're missing a receipt for the slice of 50-cent pizza you just bought, so I kept reminding myself, through my wine and grappa, to be sure to ask for a receipt on my way out. As luck would have it, my timing was from hell. I went to pay (remember there was no bill) just as the police chief passed heading for the WC, so I paid and asked in a loud, firm voice for *lo scontrino,* a receipt. The police chief looked up and, recognizing me from town, put his arm around my shoulder and smiled.

"What receipt?" he said. Then, nodding toward the owner, added, "we're friends."

Only in Italy.

~

After lunch went back to my beams. We sorted them by size, using the crane, and I tried to match the ones that went in the same room, trying to remember which beam I chose for where. At the bottom of the pile was a gem. It was an extraordinary beam, a foot and a half across, ancient, roughly hewn, with something I'd never seen: a fork at one end where the trunk of the oak had branched off in a Y. It would be perfect in the long hallway that joined the entrance and salon. I worked for days cleaning it, measuring it, cutting it to length, and deciding which side to turn up, which end would look best where. It was ready. Our first beam. A thrilling moment: we were actually beginning to build the house.

Everyone helped. Asea ran the crane, Fosco and Georgi were on a scaffold ready to set the beam in place, and Alessandro and Piero held guy ropes from both ends so the beam would not swing loose and batter our walls to rubble. Camera in hand, I was busy pouring sweat. The beam swung high over the top wall and began its slow decent. It was majestic. As we lowered it into place, everyone clapped. Then we took away the scaffold to have a better look. It was a showpiece. But Fosco was quiet and I felt uneasy. We went home. The party seemed to have ended before it began.

When I arrived the next morning they were all in the hallway silently staring at the beam. I looked up. It looked as if the Goodyear blimp had landed in the house.

"It's too big, right?" I asked.

No one said no.

Asea turned on the crane, and we hooked on the wire and guy ropes and yanked out the magnificent forked beam and dumped it on the ground.

Not all dreams look perfect in the morning.

And so it often went. We would imagine features, draw them,

and try them out and if they didn't work, we tore them out and started all over again. Slowly we were going broke. I decided Buster and Candace would come that weekend and we would pre-fit each beam, try it in place, turn it, and number it so they'd be ready for placement Monday morning. Buster was seven then and, at four feet high, not tall enough to climb walls to set the beam in place or heavy enough to hold the guy line. So we assigned him the eighty-foot crane. It was electric, with remote controls. We first had him try it out with a branch. The kid was a natural. That weekend we managed to pre-fit every beam.

Next on our list were doors. Or, rather, addressing the lack thereof. The interior doors upstairs were hand-made, but down in the stables we needed six more. Fosco wanted to make standard-sized openings and have a carpenter make wood doors to fit. I wasn't thrilled; I didn't want new doors. I called Dante and, as I'd hoped, he had a stack of long forgotten ones.

I chose the heaviest of the lot, some so thick they could withstand a catapult. Fosco just stared, and then he called Piero. He put his arm around Piero's shoulder and said with a forced calm, "the *dottore* has another new invention. Instead of building a stone house and cutting a piece of wood to fit the hole, we're going to knock down the stones and build the house around a door."

Piero blinked hard.

18 ~ THE HUMAN ARMAGEDDON

*T*he time arrived to prepare the land for vines. Well before the destruction of Il Colombaio, Candace, Buster, and I had begun clearing the brambles from the olives. With shears and sickles and machetes, we cleaned almost two hundred olives in the ten acres below the house. At one time there had been a cultivated olive grove but most of the ancient trees died off in the devastating frost of 1984. The rest Banfi cut down, intending to plant vines. When the vine planting was shelved, the broad trunks sprouted shoots that grew into ten-foot trees. I asked the neighbors, who all had olives, what they thought of transplanting mine. The response was unanimous: If you move them they'll all die, so dig them up and burn them. But, as usual, I had my own plan.

Along the road I had seen a slight, serious-faced man with thinning grey hair, delicately operating an enormous excavator. I stopped and asked him what he would think of transplanting the olives to form a dense grove around the house. His eyes lit up. "It would make a beautiful oasis," he said. Although we worked together every day for the next month moving the olive forest, that was about all that Constantino had to say.

Monday morning I heard the tracks of a machine rattling up the drive, but it wasn't the big excavator; it was an even larger front-end loader. The excavator, he explained, would have required dangling a rope from the bucket and tying it around the root-ball of each tree and lifting it from the ground. Then we'd swing it the few hundred yards to its new home. With all that movement the soil would fall from the roots, the root hairs would dry out, and the rope would strip the bark from all the trunks. The trees would never survive. Instead, the loader's great wide bucket would slip in below the roots, lift the tree, root ball and all, and place it— intact—down a pre-dug ramp into the new hole.

This work demanded superhuman patience and exactitude from Constantino. He couldn't just drive, ram, and dump. The old stumps and the new trees in them were so frail and so spread out that he had to watch and follow my hand signals to the inch. Too much push and the stump would fall to bits, tearing apart the root-ball and the young trees. Too little push and the ball would fall apart as he lifted it. Placing was equally problematic. He would bring the tree down the ramp and, as gingerly as putting an egg on marble, he'd deposit the root ball, with the trunks of the new trees as vertical as possible. Once set down, there was no adjusting. With a hand shovel, I would simply fill in beneath the root-ball to be sure the tree remained upright.

The neighbors came by, watched, and shook their heads. "It's good you have the loader here," they said, "so you can dig them up and bury them all when they're dead."

But Constantino and I persevered. Of the two hundred olives we moved, all survived. And within a month we had an oasis of olives encircling the house.

~

The land around the old olives had not been tilled for decades. It was so hard, you could cut bricks from it. Fabrizio insisted that the whole field be loosened and turned at least three feet down to give the new vines a chance to grow deep fast.

The machine to loosen the soil was the size of a small house. Using a single enormous tooth that towered over my head, it gouged for days. Then a similar sized plough was attached, which turned the soil from what seemed like the center of the earth. Fossils emerged. There were shells of every kind, skeletons of strange fish and bits of human bone, even half a cranium. The fields were ready, but they would have to lie fallow until the spring to let the sun and frost crumble and fine the soil and the earth settle. If we planted now, it would sink around the frail roots and choke them.

In the meantime, we cleaned and thinned the edges of the woods bordering the field to give the coming vines more room to breathe. For this, we hired Alvaro. Little did we know he was The Human Armageddon.

Alvaro was fifty, smiling, and dangerous. He could take a simple task like turning around a tractor in a ten-acre field into a national disaster. His first near homicide involved Giancarlo.

Giancarlo is our personal angel. He lives with his wife, son, shrill mother-in-law and voluntarily deaf father-in-law in Tavernelle, so he's always close enough to come and save our lives. He is the world's most gentle, undemanding, and indefatigable man. He retired early from the municipality where he did maintenance for years and came by way of Heaven to work with us.

Alvaro and Giancarlo were thinning the trees along the edges of the fields. Alvaro cut them down with a chainsaw and Giancarlo then hacked limbs and branches with the *penata,* a short machete. The nature of his work called for Giancarlo always to have his head down, so his life depended on Alvaro yelling *"Attento!"* to get out of the way. And Alvaro did just that, only with a three-second delay. He'd finish cutting a tree, watch it topple, the top branches entombing Giancarlo, then he'd yell at top of his voice, *"Attento!"*

Second of Alvaro's deadly events was his own near suicide. We had a brand new tractor. It was small in order to work the narrow rows of the densely planted vines Fabrizio demanded. To work the hills, it had wide steel tracks and a fiberglass roof to give the driver shade. Alvaro was to go through the freshly plowed fields, with a cart in tow, and remove any remaining bits of the olive stumps because, if left, the rotted stumps would leave bad acids in the soil, inhibiting root growth and adding odd flavors to the grapes.

How or why Alvaro got to the edge of the cliff, we'll never know. I was nailing *correnti* to the beams in the tower when I heard Candace yelling, "Chum! Armageddon!" I had Asea send me the crane's bucket to get me down quickly.

"I'm not panicking," she blurted. "But isn't Alvaro supposed to be picking roots in the fields? So why did he just take the chainsaw toward the cliff?"

I ran, but not in time. I heard the saw scream, a tree crash, and then an awful grinding sound.

The cart was still on solid ground but one track of the little tractor was hanging over the cliff. The only thing that kept it from hurtling down below was a young oak supporting the fiberglass roof. Alvaro revved the chainsaw and began to cut the oak. I grabbed him from behind. Outraged, he yelled, "I'm saving the tractor. That tree is scratching the roof."

I couldn't breathe. I yanked the saw out of his hand. "Get on the tractor," I ordered.

"But I'll die."

"You'll die anyway if I chainsaw you in half!" I pulled the trigger and the saw roared.

He scampered on.

"Put it in reverse."

"But the roof . . ."

I pulled the trigger again.

He yanked the gear level and the little tractor crawled obediently on one chain, scraping the paint from the roof, but edging bit by bit, at a shallow angle, back onto solid ground.

I should have fired him then. Or if not then, then right after he ran the chainsaw without oil until it turned white with heat and fused into a solid block. Or after, pivoting around and around on a pointed rock, he tore one of tracks right off the tractor. Instead I waited until he moved my car, forgot the handbrake, and turned it into an accordion.

19 ~ VINEMAN

*U*nlike most things in life, revenge is both non-fattening and fun. Immediate revenge, however, should be avoided for, much like impulse shopping, you miss out on all the joy of planning falling bricks, or tying shoelaces together at the top step of the leaning tower of Pisa.

By now I had mentally drowned the Roman usurer in one of his giant barrels of wine, or, as one neighbor actually did to another who slept with his wife, taken electric pruning shears and cut the man's favorite vineyard to the ground. Luckily, fate and a load of pig shit did all the work for me.

Not long after we shook hands on Il Colombaio with Rivella and Bucci, the Roman shyster showed up at our door. He had heard rumors that we were thinking of moving from La Marinaia, and he hoped they weren't true because he had the deal of a lifetime for us. These were dire times during the corruption trials, and word had it he and his winery were on the ropes, so his consortium, which owned not only the vineyard on our doorstep but also the lake and the thirty acres of fields surrounding us—all potentially excellent vineyards—was in selling mode. I had asked Piccardi once to appraise the whole package. He estimated that it would be a steal at $150,000.

The Roman spoke so fast I could hardly catch a word. Then he slowed down and announced, as if talking to the deaf, "one hundred and fifty thousand American dollars." He held his breath. I smiled and didn't say a word. Thinking he had me, he shot out his hand. *"D'accordo?"* he blurted.

"Seventy-five," I said.

"How can you say that? You'd be stealing it."

"Sixty-five," I said.

"You just said seventy-five!"

"The market crashed since then."

He got angry. "Fine! I won't even give it to you for $150,000 now."

"Sixty," I said.

His face twitched. I held out my hand. "Fifty-five," I said. "I was only going to pay fifty but since we're friends and neighbors."

"How about seventy-five?" he pleaded.

"How about fifty?" I said.

"You're a thief."

That evening I phoned Candace's brother and told him I got him half the valley for a song. He was thrilled.

"I'll send a check by courier," he said.

I lay in bed that night with a big grin on my face.

~

But the Roman also dreamt of sweet revenge. After the deal was signed, he confronted me, smiling. "It's crazy for you to buy a tractor for those few vines, why don't you let me rent the vineyard back for a year until you can plant more."

We agreed on a good price: four hundred bottles of his Vino Nobile de Montepulciano. I asked if we could leave them in his cellars, for we had no ideal space where the temperature was even. He consented, but when the year was up, he laughingly wouldn't pay.

That's when fate sent pig shit. I noticed on the map that our new property line passed within five feet of a house on the Roman's other land. It had been handsomely renovated for guests, including a huge reception room. One morning I saw workers rushing about, unloading vases of plants and flowers. They told me it was a big gala that night for foreign journalists and buyers to come and taste their wines. This was my big chance. In wine tasting, the nose is as important as the mouth, so I phoned Bonari, who had two hundred pigs at the bottom of the valley. *Emergenza!* I said. "I need a load of fresh pig shit tonight."

"Fine," he said. "Where do I dump it?"

"Beside the lake," I said. "Five feet from the Roman's house."

"Why not on it?" he suggested.

"I'm not cruel," I said.

That night we could barely sleep from the smell of pig

shit drifting down from a quarter mile away.

~

Pierre Guillaume resembles Alain Prost, the revered Formula One driver of the nineties: lean, small, quick, French. He is Europe's most respected nurseryman for vine rootstock. He marched through our fields as if he were attacking the Bastille, writing notes on maps, on the soil engineer's report, and then on his pack of cigarettes. He was choosing vine clones for each field. Poor Fabrizio huffed and puffed behind us.

"In each field," Guillaume instructed, "we will plant at least three different clones. That way the wine will have more complexity, more finesse."

On the way back, I took them past the abandoned Etruscan terraces where Rivella had said we could make a world-famous Syrah. The stone retaining walls had crumbled long ago from running water and from deer and wild boar climbing over them on the way down to the creek. Guillaume studied the paths they had cut, kicked the dirt and picked up samples, even took a small piece and tasted it. Then he studied the course of the sun, felt the breeze, and announced, "149 and 101 Polsen for rootstock," and reeled off a bunch of clones. In atypically undiplomatic language, he added, "if you don't plant Syrah here, I will."

Fabrizio beamed. We had our fourth grape varietal: full house. Madhouse.

~

127

On Fabrizio's command we began cleaning the upper fields. Since they had been abandoned for decades, some of the trees that grew in them had reached substantial size. I had never before owned even a bit of forest—La Marinaia had only a tall hedge, an enormous poplar, the toothpick walnuts, and the few dozen little olives we planted, but nothing you could look at with awe. So when it came to clear the fields I was determined to save a bush here and a sapling there. I even wanted to save a patch of ivy. I was driving Constantino crazy. I had him using a twenty-ton machine as if it were a pair of tweezers. Through a complex set of hand-signals and facial expressions I would explain to him how to swerve, which plants to avoid, and which ones to uproot. The signal for the last was my hand across my throat.

The first few days my hand always said "stop" or "swerve," but by week's end it was always slicing across my neck. The only survivors were a few big ilexes, which we dug up, dragged down and replanted at the house, and a giant oak that, against everyone's advice, I left standing in the exact center of a vineyard. I had morphed from a save-every-leaf ninny into Ferenc the Hun.

20 ~ RICCARDO THE GHOST

*A*nd then there was the day we buried Gioia alive.

Tuscans are known to be pig-headed and fiercely independent, but Gioia takes the cake. We had to duct the water from the spring down to the house, a distance of more than half a mile. A ditch had to be dug for the pipe, and to avoid going uphill we had to go through dense woods. Not wanting to cut any trees, I decided that the ditch had to be dug by hand. It would be a few weeks' work, requiring not only someone dedicated, but also a loner who, throughout the long days, would not miss company. Gioia was recommended on both counts. He was small, wiry, silent, a bit bent over, and he never smiled—which is why he was nicknamed Gioia, meaning joy. A brilliant mechanic, he could fix anything with almost nothing, until he learned to fly in a machine of his own invention.

As the story goes, he wanted to fly all his life but never had the money for lessons or expensive rentals, so he decided to go flying on his own. He built himself a helicopter out of a child's swing set, a lawnmower, and a chair. The village of Sant' Angelo Scalo stopped by his shop daily to watch him cut, weld, re-cut, and weld again. The contraption grew. It was simple, light, and in every way sensible except for the attachment of the motor. Gioia was smart enough to realize that there would be excessive vibration and turbulence. So when he attached the engine to the frame, made of the swing-set and chair, he did it with flexible mounts, and connected the final attachment to the most flexible mount of all: himself. He hauled the rig over to the soccer field, sat down, and strapped in. He started the engine. The town watched, the rotors spun, the town stepped back, and Gioia flew. At first he hovered just above the ground, doing small figure eights, then he pulled the lever for more gas. The engine roared and Gioia rose, like a dust devil, toward the heavens. The town broke into a unanimous cheer; they had their own da Vinci. Some say he was as high as the steeple, others swear he'd flown right out of sight, when from above, where the roar had been, now came an ominous silence. Then down came Gioia. Fast.

He wasn't in the hospital long, but they say he was never the same again. Nowadays he liked to work alone. He spent the mornings digging the ditch in the woods, laying the pipe, burying small wells at all the high points and installing valves that would let out the trapped air. After lunch, he slept. He would find himself a warm corner in the sun, protected from the wind, sometimes in the courtyard, or by the stairs, or in the doorway of the cellar. There he'd curl up and snooze.

One cold, blustery afternoon, we finished walling in a space that would hold the stainless steel liner of the chimney for the furnace. At quitting time we looked for Gioia. His three-wheel truck was still there, so we began shouting toward the woods. No response. I had Asea hoist me up in the bucket of the crane so my voice would carry farther, and I bellowed. Still no Gioia, until Piero heard a whimper from the furnace room, behind the freshly mortared wall.

The next day Gioia finished laying the tube and attached it to the ancient stone cistern behind the house. Then he hiked back to the spring and opened up the valve. Nothing came but air. We waited. More air and then bits of dirt. Finally there was a sad trickle. Then with a burst, as if celebrating its escape, came a spurt of water, muddy and frothy, but it soon ran clear, tumbling and splashing into the cistern. Gioia had brought water to the oasis.

~

Il Colombaio had begun to look like a house again. At ground level the subfloor with the airspace had been poured. On the first floor, the beams, *correnti* and *mezzane* were in. A steel web was laid over that, which was also let into the walls, then covered with three inches of cement. New laws required all houses to be earthquake-proof, so the very tops of all the walls were hollowed out, and a rebar beam was made in one continuous piece all the way around and concrete poured over it.

The roof was solid insulation over the *mezzane*, then more steel mesh and concrete, waterproofing, and finally old roof tiles. We replaced the chipped and broken ones with Dante's.

Finally, one December morning, with snow clouds piling up against the volcano, my stiff fingers put the last roof tile in place. Il Colombaio was more solid than it had ever been. If it made it through seven centuries with only mice and mortar in its walls, it should now stand a thousand years built with steel and cement.

That night I slept as I hadn't slept all year.

~

Whenever you tell yourself, "I'll just do one more thing and then stop," that's the time to lie down on the ground.

Since the outside of the house was so close to being finished, I thought it appropriate to clean up the unused beams that lay in a pile at the entrance to the courtyard. It seemed easy. I'd simply tie the crane's cable to them, haul them high, and swing them away, up the hill, out of everybody's way. Child's play; I'd seen my own kid do it.

The problem was it was getting dark so I had to hurry. Instead of doing the wise thing by moving one beam at a time, I thought I'd be a tough guy and move them all at once. I slipped the cable under them as well as I could, looped it over, and slid on the hook. Then I picked up the control box.

It's a simple device with only six buttons, four for

lateral direction and two for up and down. I had never worked it before, but there's a first time for everything. I pushed the middle button and, "whirr," I watched the big beams rise. Proud of myself, I smiled. I was lifting them high to swing over the house when two beams started to slip out of the cable right above the roof. I panicked and pushed a button. "Whirr," the beams headed for the tower. Another button, "whirr," the beams headed for a wall. Button, "whirr," beams swung away directly for my car. I swung them wildly back, smart move, but stopped with a sudden jolt and now, with the long fetch, the beams swung on their own—a battering ram with ten arms.

I took a deep breath and pushed another button. *Porca troia della Madonna gonfiata, quella ignorante puttana.* Some sadistic maniac had made a seventh button that read, in microscopic letters, "FAST."

Bam! Down came my workshop roof. Bam! Down came the crumbling courtyard wall. Bam! Demolished the steel drum that held water. Bam! Down came the pigsty, which I never liked at all. Bam! An oak tree toppled on the hill. On the last swing I pushed "down" and dumped them in the well. I tried to lift them out but they were stuck.

Fosco came around the corner and looked at me askance.

"Bull's eye," he said.

~

The second best part of having the roof on was that we could finally have that Tuscan tradition—the roofing party. Most people take the masons, architect, and builder to a restaurant, but we wanted the event to be as unforgettable for everyone as it would be for us, so we rented the great hall at Banfi Castle.

Today the Castle houses a Michelin-starred restaurant, but back then there was just the vast empty room with Riccardo the Ghost, who died in 1310, as its only tenant. A few times a year, Banfi would host a gala evening for special clients or journalists, with Tommi's wife, Maria, an excellent cook, preparing the meals. She once had a restaurant in the region of Abruzzo, where she added a gourmet twist to classic country dishes. We were truly flattered when she agreed to cook the private feast for us.

We imagined something simple, but when we arrived, we couldn't believe our eyes. The great hall was set with linen, silver, and china, and lit only by candlelight. In front of each place setting were six chalice-sized wine glasses, one for each of Banfi's exceptional wines, plus a champagne flute. Feeling touched and a bit out of place, the fourteen of us stood there and downed the champagne while Maria told the story of poor Riccardo who lives in the tower but roams at night. At that point there was a howl, and Buster, now eight, who had always wanted to be a knight, ran and grabbed the sword from the suit of armor in the corner. He yelled *"Andiamo,* Riccardo! I'm not afraid." But, just to be sure, he ducked in behind Candace. We laughed right through our first glass of Banfi chardonnay, which accompanied a vast assortment of salamis and *mortadellas*. The most intriguing of the pastas was *maccheroni alla chitarra* made with a tomato sauce in which chunks of carrots, celery, onions, and pork simmer all morning and are then removed, leaving only a blend of intense scents and flavors. Next was *agnello brodoristretto*, lamb stew topped with a whipped egg and lemon, followed by a powerfully flavored *arosticera*, bits of sheep grilled on skewers. Lastly Maria brought out *crostata di ricotta*, a pie that went wonderfully with Banfi's flowery and exotic Moscadello.

Give a Tuscan food and wine, and he'll be loud and boisterous even in his grave. We joked and talked about the horrors of the first six months of rebuilding Il Colombaio, when after four or five appetizers, and seven or eight bottles of wine, we noticed Buster was missing. We assumed he was with Maria and her helpers, but when Candace went to check, both of them were gone. From behind us came a triumphant yell. The door to the tower opened and out walked Maria and Buster holding the sword. "We chased Riccardo out," Buster announced. "He'll never come again."

It was well past midnight when we filed out, so full of food and wine that even Piccardi was quiet. The masons had all left, as had the kitchen ladies, and even Tommi said he had to go to pick up their daughter from a dance, so only we and Maria remained, to tidy up, turn off the lights, and lock up the castle. All was dark and silent as we crossed the empty courtyard, talking softly in the moonlight, when, from the highest window in the tower, out hung Riccardo twisting and howling like a deranged banshee—under a tablecloth.

Buster clung to Candace and turned paler than the moon.

~

With Gioia's aqueduct in place, we could plant trees to our hearts' content.

Just down the road, some mature olive trees came up for grabs so we began landscaping in earnest long before the house was done. Most of our neighbors were planting still more vines, but since their fields were limited, they could only do so by cutting down old, magnificent but unproductive olives. Constantino and I offered to save them the trouble of cutting, burning, digging up the stump, and hauling it away—we would come with our loader and transplant them all.

Our own olives we had set in a ring well away from the house, leaving space for a future lawn, shrubs, shade trees, and flowers. Into this area we now introduced century-old olives, whose gnarled and tortured trunks alone were sculptures to behold. We were almost finished transplanting our ninth old beauty when a young man came and introduced himself as Pietro, a *vivaista*, the owner of a nearby nursery. He'd heard that I was obsessed with trees, so he came because he had dozens of mature Mediterranean pines and some big cypresses he had to get rid of to plant a field of small ones. If I just paid for the hauling and planting I could have them for next to nothing.

I gave Pietro free rein in what to plant, so around the house and cistern we had more clumps of cypresses than a cemetery. When he finished I asked him for the bill.

There is something one must learn in Tuscany: the only thing more difficult than getting someone to come and work is extracting the bill at labor's end. Most people congenially say "later" and then vanish, only to show up in a year, when you haven't a penny to your name. So Pietro grudgingly walked around, counted the trees he'd planted, and then handed me a slip of paper.

The prices were as agreed but there was a mistake. "You forgot the two big elms," I said.

"Those are a gift," he said.

"For what?" I said.

"For liking my trees so much."

Seeing I was touched by his gesture he said, "Look, Máté, many people are mistrustful and suspicious, convinced that I will somehow cheat them. I can sense this. So I pad the bill now and then.

"For those who trust me, I'll work day and night, lose sleep, lose my shirt just to see their faces when I plant something they love. Those things I remember. You know what it's like to go back after ten years and see what has become of a little tree you planted?" And he waved his hand and fell silent, as if emotions like that could never be explained.

21 ~ CHRISTMAS IN
THE DOLOMITES

*I*t seems no matter what you expect, life will always throw you the opposite. I was sure I would feel satisfaction from having the walls reinforced and the roof back on. Now that Il Colombaio was solid and safe, I thought I would just coast and enjoy filling in smaller details until it was finished. Instead, I woke up one morning with nothing left: no passion for the drive, no yearning for the laughter and banter of the masons or the five-course lunch at Trattoria Sciame. Worse, I had a deadline for a book that required a mind not overloaded with drainpipe diameters or the ideal septic tank size, so I decided to do what I do best: I escaped.

I was born in the most mountainous and romantic part of Hungary: Transylvania. After the war, we lost the mountains to Romania. The borders were tightly guarded. We had to escape at night to get back to what was still left of our nation. At one year old, I rode in my dad's backpack while he walked over the mountains.

When I was ten, the Hungarians got sick of living under Soviet terror. We rebelled and kicked their army out for six glorious days. But they came back with bombers and two thousand tanks. All we had were rifles and bottles filled with gasoline. My mother and her beau took part in the fighting. He headed the distribution of food to the rebels, so we had to escape again, this time to Austria. We walked for two days and two nights, in snow, fog, and ice.

The escape from Tuscany would be to recharge what braincells I had left and to spend a couple of weeks finishing the book. The Piccardis had taken us skiing in the snowy Dolomites for a *settimana bianca*, white week, the year before, and as with most beautiful places I visit, I was ready to stay forever.

The Dolomites are perhaps the most dramatic mountains on earth. Sharp and craggy, they were, until the war, a part of Austria's most beautiful region: Tyrol. It still is a place of meticulously-kept villages comprised of Hansel-and-Gretel houses and tall-steepled churches, men in *Lederhosen*, tortuous hillsides where the hay is cut by hand, alpine pastures full of the sound of cowbells, and of a wonderful blend of Austrian and Italian cuisine. It is the home of hearty, lively, people who love music and dancing, and for whom climbing a ten-thousand-foot peak is no more taxing than strolling across a park would be for me.

~

The town of San Vigilio in Marebbe in the heart of the

Dolomites is at the end of a terrifying road etched into a bluff above a river. Until the 1960s, there was no way in but on footpaths that wound through the woods and fields from hamlet to hamlet. Here and there, where the view was good, or where water sprouted from a spring into a hollowed out log trough, there would be a bench to rest, and maybe a raised altar carved of wood, with a sprig of heather or wild azalea tucked in beside Jesus.

The town of six hundred is nestled in a tiny valley, with steep mountains all around. They are part of a vast natural reserve with too many rugged peaks to name, so the highest ones are called Nove and Dieci, Nine and Ten. In winter, the peaks and the town are buried in snow. According to Tommi Bucci, this is Italy's best skiing.

The Piccardis left early that year, but we stayed a few more days, and after skiing I wandered the footpaths beaten in the snow. Near a pass between two peaks I found a one-man sawmill: a sliding bed and blade, and Josef, the man who owned it. He was as sinewy as mountain men come, with shining eyes and a shy demeanor. He spoke with a strong accent—the first language here is Ladino (based on ancient Latin), the second German, and only the third Italian—and was at first hesitant when I asked him if there might be something humble one could rent year-round for skiing, climbing, and writing. But when I told him I was from Canada, where I lived for years at Whistler Mountain in the Rockies, he began to treat me like a long-lost friend.

"I do have a place," he said. "Although you might be

too tall for it."

We wound down the hill to where, behind the woods, a handful of rooftops showed. There were three houses in the hamlet, three barns, a small stone shed, and a chapel. Wooden fences guarded vegetable gardens now covered with snow. The bottoms of the houses were made of stone, the upper floors of larice, of the cedar family, a wood that turned dark over the centuries. Two of the houses were perfectly kept, but the last one was a bit wild. We went to it. In the entrance, a ceiling-high brick oven blasted heat. We climbed a set of stairs into the attic, all pale pine: the walls, ceilings, floors, and even the beams that held the roof.

"Watch your head," Josef cautioned just as he heard the thud. Two small bedrooms opened toward a barn; an eat-in kitchen and the living room faced the valley, mountains, and sky. From the small, covered balcony you felt you could fly. The rent was the same as we paid in Paris to store the car. We shook hands. That was the lease agreement for the year.

And so we packed up our clothes in Tuscany to spend a few weeks over Christmas at the top of the world.

~

The trip started well. Weighed down with skis and presents our car didn't slip and slide, as was its custom in the rain, but then just south of Florence the sky grew black and it began to snow. At the last exit to Florence the traffic stood still. For those who love to drive, the road from there to Bologna is a real Grand Prix circuit; there is no straight piece of road for almost fifty miles. It dips, climbs, curves, and dives into tunnels, then bursts out onto slippery, tight viaducts. There are some—without naming names—who just can't resist driving it with zeal. It's pure fun when dry, a thriller in the rain, and completely impassible in the snow. We stood and waited. The radio told us the pass was closed ahead and might be for hours until the first machines got through, except the machines could not get past the cars stuck in the snow. The family was distraught, but I could hardly contain my joy; what better way to begin a vacation than a forced overnight stay in my beloved Florence?

I backed down the shoulder to the exit. Over the years I had fallen for a small rambling hotel, now wonderfully restored, and called, naturally enough, Brunelleschi, since it was only a few steps from his dome. It looked like luxury but it was off season. With as much gumption as I could muster, I went in and asked if by chance they had special rates for refugee writers from the storm. An enormous smile broke on the manager's face.

"Would the broom closet do, Mr. Máté?" He asked. "I can let you have it at half price."

"Fine," I said. "But only if you tell me where the best food is in town."

We took our bags out of the car and began to climb. After a few flights of stairs we entered a door marked Suite Duomo.

Candace laughed out loud. One room led into another, and then another, but most magical was the view. A window in the salon framed to absolute perfection Brunellschi's unparalleled dome, and its pink, green, and white marble walls below.

We spent the afternoon climbing inside the dome and seeing Donatello's cocky little David and his frail, wooden Mary Magdalene, Botticelli's Spring and Venus and della Robbia's hilarious choirboys. The dinner at the Tre Gobbi (the three hunchbacks) was superb: fettuccini with pheasant sauce and a Bistecca Fiorentina that melted in your mouth, and, in honor of Tommi Bucci, one of Banfi's best wines: their SummuS, a delightful aromatic blend of Sangiovese, Merlot, Cabernet Sauvignon, and the prized Syrah.

That night we stayed by the window for hours, staring at the snow drifting past the marble walls and the dome. We awoke to Florence under a deep blanket of snow.

The snow around the hamlet was patchy when we arrived in the Dolomites. Our attic felt cold; Josef had neglected to feed the furnace. We put away the food, gifts, and wine, and noticed that the full bottle of grappa I had left three months before now stood empty. I went down to the cellar to feed the furnace and noticed Josef walking briskly away toward the barn. We chatted amicably, and then I mentioned the empty bottle.

"That's grappa for you," he said, his eyelids sagging, "If you leave the cork slightly loose, it evaporates overnight." So I prepared to feed the furnace myself three times a day for as long as we remained—or as long as Josef managed to find more grappa.

~

That night, when the cows had settled in the barn, and after the chapel bell rang, it began to snow. It fell and hid the mountains in the distance, then the village in the elbow of the valley, then the hill across the way, then the hay-shed just below. The snow fell as soft as a whisper. It snowed against the windows and piled against the door. By midnight it was up to a foot and still coming down. It snowed too beautifully to sleep.

I tucked in the family, turned out the lights, and went out into the night. The snow fell in lazy flakes against my face and settled like a light hand on my shoulder. The cows breathed heavy in the darkness of the barn. Further up the ridge, I turned and looked back down. The snow drifted in curtains like thick lace, and down below the half-buried hamlet slept. The only light came through a window of the chapel, where someone had lit a candle.

~

Two days before Christmas we were still without a tree. I asked Josef where we could buy one and he laughed. "The mountain is covered with them. There's a saw in the shed."

His brother Toni, standing nearby, tried to say something, but his stutter wouldn't let him form the word. He was younger than Josef, maybe forty, and round, with cheeks as red as if stained by Merlot. He wore short leather pants year round, acknowledging a change in the season only by rolling down his socks. His career was to get by. Their father left the house to them, the vegetable garden fed them, and the two unmarried sisters next door cooked for them, so their needs were minimal at best. In the winter he ski-patrolled, in the spring he fixed the trails, in the summer he rested, and in autumn he padded his meager savings by being the acknowledged *porcini*-hunting champion of the valley.

Through September he would leave in the dead of night, not because he had far to go—the *porcini* fields were nearby—but so no one could follow him and learn his secret places. By the time we would rise to begin our daily climb, Toni would be coming back through the fields, his boots soaked, his shirt drenched through, and dangling from both hands were wicker baskets brimming with *porcini*. By noon he'd have sold every last one to the restaurants and hotels in town. We begged to buy some but he refused. He gave them to us as presents, always stuttering to say that this way he was less weighed down.

After lunch, Buster and I went to find a tree. We got the handsaw and headed downhill toward the old mill where, on the edge of a clearing, we had seen some saplings growing. But we didn't get far. Toni was coming up the rise, his naked knees pushing snow, dragging behind him the fullest blue spruce I have ever seen. He grinned and decided it was no use trying to talk so he handed Buster the tree, tipped his hat, and turned and disappeared into the woods.

By Christmas Eve, the snow was up to the window of the barn, where the heat from the cows melted a round dent in the drift. The full moon was so bright you had to squint. It seemed an offense against the silence to use the car, so we donned our ski clothes, laced our hiking boots, and took the ancient footpath to midnight mass in town. The woods bowed under the white blanket, and we wound down, over the narrow bridges that crossed chasms, along fields, past silent barns, and past the carved wooden Jesus that now stood deep in snow.

The church pews in Pieve are bare pine, clean and bright as if scrubbed every day, but the altar and walls are alive with hand-carved saints and angels, painted and over-laid with gold. They swoop and fly as only Baroque angels can; even the arms of the Madonna are open passionately wide.

Everyone was in their best *Lederhosen* and dark green *Loden*. Men wore heavy felt mountain hats and women lace shawls. Every seat was full. We sang and listened to the choir sing, then shook hands with our neighbors and wished them Merry Christmas. We stepped back out into the moonlight as the bells tolled, and from the mountain across the way, church bells sounded in response.

Buster, who was convinced we would miss Santa, rushed us home. We trudged and perspired and waited for Candace to catch up. The moon hung lower in the sky; the shadows had grown longer in the forest. Buster burst into the house and saw that there were still just a few presents under the tree. He breathed a sigh of relief; thank goodness Santa had not yet come. So tired he could hardly stand, he still wondered: What if Santa doesn't know we're here? What if he went to La Marinaia instead?

"Santa knows everything," Candace said.

I told him to go to bed, and not to worry because when the reindeer came he would hear their bells.

"Like cow bells?" he asked.

"No, much smaller," I said.

"Don't forget to leave him cookies and milk," he said, his voice trailing off as his head touched the pillow.

It began to snow again, this time even harder than before. Candace and I put out presents, changed into our pajamas, and turned out the lights, leaving only the ones glowing on the tree. With the chime we had bought just for this moment, I walked through the attic, ringing in the dark.

"Mom! Dad!" Buster cried leaping out of bed. "I heard the bells!"

"Me too," Candace said, and bundled him in her coat. He bolted for the tree and stood staring at all the presents, while out on the deck I rang the chime again.

"The reindeer," Buster whispered, and headed for the door.

I just had enough time to sneak into the kitchen. When I doubled back, they were already outside, the snow swirling before them.

"Look!" Buster pointed into the night. "There they are, the reindeer. Can you see them, Dad?"

Candace smiled at me.

"Aren't they beautiful," I said.

22 ~ STONES AND PEOPLE

We returned from the mountains after *La Befana*, the Day of the Witch, when in hope of a fertile spring, the Witch of Winter, made of straw, is burned in the town square.

Il Colombaio looked like a real house again. During the weeks we were gone, the masons had performed miracles inside. They'd chipped out the loose mortar between the stones and refilled and replastered the walls. When I asked why some walls were left unfinished, Fosco said he was awaiting my decision. It was then that I understood that he had an artist's soul. He had found the stones and their patterns in those walls so unusual that he thought I might want to leave them exposed. He was right, and those ten walls turned out to be the most eye-catching in the house.

The stones had bits of mortar on them, and the *mezzane* in the ceilings were flecked with paint and soot; they would need to be sandblasted to regain their virgin look. Sandblasting is a simple process: experts come in with a machine on wheels and a few dozen bags of razor-sharp silica which, if sprayed long enough at the same spot, can cut a hole to China.

They did a perfect job: the stones were clean, and the *mezzane* had taken on their original terracotta color. And here we received a wonderful surprise. Centuries ago, every village had its own kiln, where local bricks were fired. Over the years, the clay and firing methods changed, so each room had a slightly different color and texture, ranging from pale to deep red. When the ceilings and floors were demolished, everything was mixed together, so after sandblasting the ceilings looked like mosaics gone wild. I panicked. What would people say when they saw that I slipped up on such a visible point of restoration? Would I be shunned on the street? Laughed at behind my back?

"Foscooo!" I yelled. He came and looked. *"Bellissima,"* he said. "We couldn't have done better blending colors if we had spent a year planning it."

I could have kissed him.

~

Professionals should know never to leave dangerous toys where impressionable owners can get at them. If they did, the sandblaster would not have sat there staring me in the eye on that quiet Saturday morning.

Self-restraint is not one of my strong points. One would think I'd have learned from the crane fiasco to leave unfamiliar machines alone, but this was no towering crane; it was just a largish vacuum cleaner. The temptation would have made a saint break out in a sweat. It seemed simple enough. I knew the red button turned on the power, the green button fed the sand, and I had seen a wand on the end of the long hose with a trigger to open or shut off the flow.

I wanted to sandblast the rust off a wrought iron door handle I had found behind the house, a straightforward task that would take only a minute. I stood out back next to the machine and saw the hose disappear through a tiny window into the house. I wasn't about to waste my time walking all the way around to check where it ended up, so: red button, then green button—nothing to it.

I took my rusty handle and strolled around to the courtyard, where I was engulfed by a cloud of sand. Beneath the cloud, like an agitated cobra, the hose lashed and struck, with no wand or trigger at its end. Instead of running back to turn off green button, red button, or just pull the plug, I went for the snake. I circled it with a rake, trying to time its moves, but the goddamn thing was ready to do battle. It reared and struck and on one quick pass blew the cuff right off my pants.

I swung the rake with all my might but the snake was faster. Then I got smart. I hooked the rake's teeth over the hose six feet from its end, and started sliding forward. I had him. He knew it. He coughed spastically, futilely. I slid and grinned. Victory was almost mine, but a foot from the end the damned thing ran completely out of sand—and the door handle remains rusty to this day.

⁓

Our project that month was to find old floor tiles. We had saved about half from the original floors, but the rest were chipped or broken. There had been no tiles in the stables below, so we had a huge hunt ahead of us.

Most people would have shrugged their shoulders and simply bought new ones—there are some exquisite ones still made by hand—but if old beams were a must then old tiles were too. Few things in a Tuscan home catch the eye like the sensuous patina and contours of old *mezzane* worn down through centuries.

Dante didn't have an old tile to his name, but he swore he'd find me some. Within a week, his rickety truck came up the driveway carrying not only some beautifully worn *mezzane*, but, rarest of all, some square tiles from the sixteenth century.

"From where?" I asked, amazed.

"A deconsecrated chapel," he answered. "I know the priest's sister."

⁓

Ever since we started on Il Colombaio, Candace wanted to use materials found right there in our valley. For bathroom floors and walls, she wanted travertine, which we heard was quarried just over the hill, at Bagno Vignoni.

You notice three things about Mario the stonecutter right away: a huge smile, Coke-bottle glasses, and his hat: a rolled-up paper bag cleverly folded at two corners. His shop roars with blades cutting and polishing the stone he hews out of the mountain. I had just begun to explain what we more or less wanted when he interrupted me.

"I know just what you need." If he'd said he could see it in my eyes, I swear I would have set his paper hat on fire.

His small quarry was a rock collector's dream, its sides glowing with the most alluring colors of strong-veined travertine. Mario had brought a pail of water, and as he walked, he rubbed it on the stone and narrated.

"You have white, the most perfect travertine—few flaws, few holes, but one big drawback: boring. Then there's pink: beautiful veins, lots of tonal change, but a bit *femminuccia*," and he let his wrist go limp. "I have something rare I think you'll like."

He threw the pail of water over what first looked like ordinary stone. It glowed a deep dark brown with lighter veins and arabesques. If I had seen it in another house, I would have died of envy.

"We'll take the whole hill," Candace said.

Mario laughed. "There are two things I know in the world," he said. "My stones and people."

23 ~ ONE VINE AT A TIME

*I*t was spring; time to plant the vines.

All we needed on top of the dozen daily decisions required to finish the inside of the house—finding marble for the kitchen counter, someone to make the kitchen counter, light fixtures, bath fixtures, door handles, and cabinets—was the dozen more decisions needed to start the vineyard.

First, we had to decide on the direction of the rows. More often than not, rows follow the slope of the land to facilitate drainage. If you run across the hill, your tractor will eventually build long dams, creating puddles that delay your entry with machinery after rain, just when your vines are in greatest need of sulfur treatments to stave off oidium.

Unfortunately, as the slope below the house is slight, we had to make a choice.

A tractor needs twenty feet of space to turn around at the end of each row. In estates like ours, with numerous small fields, leaving wide strips at the ends consumes much precious land, so the fewer rows, the better. In other words, our rows would ideally be running the length of the field, not across.

Two more factors to consider in choosing row direction are sun and wind. In zones with few hours of sunshine, it's best to run north-south to ensure sun on both sides of the vines for maturation. However, these are usually the same zones that get the most rain, hence it's best to run the rows in the direction the wind blows, helping the soil and leaves dry quickly to limit fungus and mildew growth.

Now, if you think it's boring reading about this stuff, imagine making one hundred similar decisions. Fabrizio, Candace and I spent hours discussing pros and cons until he inadvertently settled it. "When you drive through the gate and up the drive, it would be beautiful to see the rows facing you, like herringbone."

This worked like a charm: the least draining part gets the most wind, the other a bit more sun.

Next, we had to decide the distance between rows and between vines. Theory has it that the ideal space between vines is one meter, or 40 inches. The problem is that to get 3,000 vines into one acre, you'd have to make the rows so tight (about 64 inches) that you'd need either a toy tractor to work it or giant machines that straddle the rows. So we settled at 72 inches between rows, with 36 inches between vines.

For our 15 acres we would need 35,000 stakes (one per plant) and 7,500 supporting poles, or one for every six plants. The questions that remained were: what length of pole, what diameter and of what material? Little wonder that in those days I kept a bottle of wine nearby.

Height of pole is critical because if the poles were too high, we would shade the bottom of one row with another, thus inhibiting equal maturation. On the other hand, if we made the poles too low, the lowest wire (where the grapes usually grow) would be so close to the ground that we'd have to hire Lilliputians to prune and pick. Apart from that, the closer the buds are to the ground, the more subject they are to frost and disease. So we made the poles five feet high, ideal for working and comfortable for gossiping with a friend in the next row.

In our area, poles were traditionally made of chestnut from the volcano, cut when the sap stopped running so they would last longest. The tip of each pole was sharpened and then set into a fire to form charcoal that would protect it from rot. But these poles tend to be thick and irregular and make passage of tractors in tight rows dangerous. Oh, please do pass the bottle.

Poles made of pine are treated with salts, which we did not want in our soil. Concrete poles are cheap but if you touch them with the tractor tracks they break. Metal poles are nice because they're galvanized and have little hooks pressed out of them so one can easily attach wires to train the vines, but they are ugly.

So we settled for acacia poles from—of all places—Hungary. These are sawn square, naturally rot-resistant, very dense, and rock-hard, so you can't drive a nail into the sons of bitches to save your life. Nail driving is no joke when you have to drive five into each of 7,500 poles, so we pre-drilled every hole and another week of my life evaporated like Josef's grappa.

~

One day Fabrizio came running across the bare fields waving a sheet of paper.

"Haven't you read your soil report," he chided. "I told you that we're low on microorganisms. Young vines need them!"

I hadn't a clue what microorganisms were but I slapped my forehead and said, "Mon Dieu! It completely slipped my mind."

"It's a good thing you have me," he grumbled. "I've ordered fifteen trucks of first-class . . . how you say *fertilisante organique?*"

"Cow shit," I offered.

Fifteen loads of manure are the size of a ski hill. For one solid week we shoveled, pitch-forked, inhaled, and walked up to our knees in shit. Our nasal passages were lined with its penetrating stench.

All this just so you can sit back in the candlelight and sip wine.

~

This was all just preparation for the real fun, which began when a truck with French license plates swung into the driveway. Inside was a mountain of white plastic bags full of our future vineyard. Guillaume is thorough. Each bag was marked with the varietal—Sangiovese, Merlot, Cabernet Sauvignon, and Syrah—plus the type of rootstock, the part that goes in the ground. Also marked was the type of clone, the part that sticks above the ground and will actually sprout the shoots. But there was a hitch: the instruction sheets ordered that the contents be kept in a refrigerated room at no more than 35 degrees Fahrenheit or they would sprout and break off as you tried to plant them. It had just rained, and the vineyards were all mud; we wouldn't be able to start for at least a week. By then, I imagined the bags would be full of grapes.

Tommi Bucci once again came to the rescue. He offered Banfi's refrigerated room for as long as we would like. I owe the man for about three generations.

~

Most modern vintners plant their vines with machines. But not the Mátés. Yet our hand planting didn't come about through affectation; there was a method to the madness. Following a laser beam projected from one end of a row, a machine can plant efficiently as long as the heads of the rows are in a straight line. If the heads of the rows curve as ours do—since we had to use every inch of our oddly shaped fields—then calculating the starting point of the machine each time takes longer than the average life. So we planted 42,000 of the little bastards by hand.

This was actually group work and almost as much fun as picking grapes. The heads of the rows were laid out, and short sticks were driven where the poles were to go later that year. A piece of wire clothesline marked every thirty-six inches was stretched down the row. The hand planting began in a most miraculous way.

But first let me tell you *what* we had to plant. The bags held eight-inch pieces of what looked to me like dry twigs with some root hairs at one end. The other end had been dipped in wax to protect it from frost. First you soak these twigs in water overnight so they can absorb enough to survive for a couple of days in the hot, dry ground. The next morning you give the sticks a haircut so that the root hairs are no longer than four inches.

Then comes the tool. It's a three-foot piece of metal with a T-shaped handle. At its bottom is a claw, something like a fine hoof. You insert a dry twig—just above the roots—into the claw, line it up with your mark on the clothes line, and lean on the T with all your might until only three inches of dry twig are showing above the ground. Then you pull up your T and the twig remains planted. Don't ask me why. You straighten the twig, straighten your back and move on down the line.

Forty-two *thousand* times.

24 ~ THE ETRUSCAN TERRACES

*N*o one likes to admit that they have a favorite child. At the outset, I liked all of our vineyards about the same. The three fields of Sangiovese near the house feel like home: the one next to Angelo's I love because of the abandoned church and steeple and it's good to drop in on Fabrizio for a chat; the one in front of the house is special because I can smell Candace's cooking in the kitchen; the one toward the cliff, which ends in Merlot, overlooks the canyon and is near enough to Fattoi's to stop in for some gossip.

Far above the house, the other fields have their own charm. The Cabernet among the oaks has a long view of the valley, and the one high in the woods looks into an overgrown castle where lives a sweet man appropriately named Castelli, who, according to Ofelio, is *"dolce come il pane,"* sweet as bread.

The distant Sangiovese vineyard by the spring is a refuge. Separated from the world by woods, you can sit under the regal oak we left in its middle and gaze far away. Three castles loom in the distance: Arginaccio, a twelfth-century tower, Argiano, a vast sixteenth-century structure, famed for having a different window for each day of the year, and, behind a row of cypresses, Banfi castle, in whose tower Riccardo lurks.

From here, we can circle back through the woods, then through an olive grove, along the canyon, into my favorite vineyard of all: the old Etruscan terraces, where we planted the Syrah.

Rebuilding the terraces with an excavator was almost as difficult as rebuilding Il Colombaio. Fosco calculated that over the year and a half of construction, we built, tore down, and then built again at least ten percent of the house, because we felt it didn't look as good as it should or could. The renovation of the terraces for Syrah followed the same pattern.

Rino was almost seventy and nearly deaf from working an excavator all his life. He loved a challenge, but when he saw the eroded terraces his smile faded. "Madonna, Máté," he gasped. "Will we leave here alive?"

The terraces were etched into a curving hillside almost too steep to climb. Most of the Etruscan walls had crumbled long ago, and pampas grass with blades as sharp as knives and a few *corbezzoli* were reclaiming them for their own. Because the terraces had been built by hand and varied in width as the slope changed, it looked as though we too would end up working them by hand. This would have bankrupted us, so we had to figure out a way of re-doing them from scratch.

Candace and I spent a week as engineers. With a tripod level and a fifteen-foot stick, we calculated the rise in five spots of varied slopes, and tried a hundred times to get the ideal heights with the minimum width so as to preserve the hand-worked look and leave no trace that a machine had ever passed.

We finally settled on six narrow terraces, each eight feet wide, with two rows of vines, one a foot from the bottom of the slope, the other a foot from the suddenly-dropping edge, with just enough space between them for our little tractor. Everything worked out fine on paper, but a pencil is no match for a twenty-ton excavator, nor does paper compare to mounds of dirt sliding into the canyon.

First we cleared the scrub by hand. We hacked down the high broom and pampas and burned them. Then, one morning, Rino eased his big machine onto the topmost terrace. For weeks he scratched and scraped, ripping up roots and rocks and leveling as he went, making sure that the long, curved terrace would have no dips where water could stand, soak the hill, and start a slide. Once he had the first terrace shaped, he went back and pounded down the slope below it. We seeded the slope with wild grasses and covered it with straw to protect the seeds from fierce sun or pouring rain. Then we moved on to the next.

I hiked up to visit him twice each morning and twice in the afternoon, not only to reassure him that his work was flawless, but to keep him company, so he wouldn't feel—as he complained one day—"like an abandoned dog."

He worked his giant bucket as though it were a hand. We never again used the surveying gear. We measured the width with a stick, the rest we just judged by eye—if it looked beautiful, it was fine.

At the third terrace we ran into rocks. Rino lost his smile. We dug and moved rocks, moved dirt then dug some more. It took nearly a month to create enough land for two thousand vines. But what vines! And what intense flavor in those grapes. Syrah is, by nature, parsimonious with its yield, and on our hot, southern slopes—our *Côte Rôti*—it's at its frugal best. The grapes are seldom bigger than blueberries, and the weight of a cluster rarely exceeds three ounces. Our one acre of Syrah has yet to yield nine hundred bottles a year, but what it lacks in quantity it makes up in concentrated flavors, which amaze everyone who tastes it.

I'm not sure why this vineyard is my favorite—perhaps because there is so little of it, or because the terraces hang precariously from the hill. Or perhaps because I love to sit at the marble table above the terraces, where in the winter the heat rising makes it feel like July. Or perhaps it's the intoxicating solitude of the steep, lush canyon and the sun beating down deep into the silence.

Whenever I need to escape, I hike up past the big cistern where Gioia's water runs, through the woods and across olives, up to my table where the world is far below, barely outlined in the mist. I sit and gaze or close my eyes and dream.

Most of the year I hear the brook, its sound bouncing

from the rock walls of its canyon.

~

When we bought Il Colombaio, we had no idea that either the brook or the canyon came with it.

The detailed map that Tommi gave us showed no heights or contours in the land. It did show a twisting line marked Fosso del Banditone, the Ditch of the Bandit, about half a mile from where Ofelio found the spring, but then every drainage ditch in Tuscany is called a *fosso* even if its high water never wets your ankles. So we assumed our *fosso* to be no different than the others, until one day when Buster was at school, Candace and I tried to bushwhack across the southern hill. The boar path we followed was scree, and we slipped and fell. We grabbed the pampas grass as we went down and our palms bled from the gashes. The boar path stopped at a boar's nest—a dry spot under an ilex. The grass was flattened where they slept. We tried to escape into the woods but slipped and kicked loose rocks, disturbing a sleeping viper.

"Terrific," Candace said. "We get bit here and we die."

She was right. You only have a half hour after a viper bite to get to the antiserum. It would have taken that long to hike out even if we knew where we were going, which we didn't. But the viper was *in letargo*, hibernating, so it just slithered away, a bit annoyed, under another stone. Since we had no luck going up, we tried going down. Once you slide on scree, it's very hard to stop; it's best to dig in your heels and just enjoy the ride. We came to a halt down below the remnants of a wall. Doves cooed and wood pigeons rustled and took flight. The air was so warm here it seemed another climate. Only when the pigeons left did we hear the water. It sounded loud, like cataracts, right below us, and there was a louder rumble somewhere up the valley.

"A waterfall," Candace blurted.

"In Tuscany?" I scoffed. "We're just north of the Sahara."

"Look, Hunky," Candace said. "The noise is water. Water makes noise when it falls. So you put the two words together and you get 'water—fall.' *Capisci?*"

Women think they know everything.

"I'll bet you my half of everything we own," I insisted.

"You bet that away years ago."

"Fine. Ten Lira."

"Fine."

Right below us the pampas grass was so dense we couldn't see where to put our feet, so we cut across the slope following a trail some small animal had made. When it turned down we continued. I led with Candace right behind, gathering speed, sliding, then through a copse of woods toward a blast of light, so thrilled with the descent I almost went over the edge. At my feet the sandstone bluff fell plumb into a canyon, and down in the gloom maybe a hundred feet below, a ribbon of smooth water shot over the edge and cascaded onto big rocks in the sun.

"Water." Candace said. "Fall."

~

The bluff was sheer all along, so we turned up-creek to find a descent. We crossed the crumbled terraces hand-in-hand. I used a fallen limb to beat down the scrub, and we ended up on a trail that had once been wide enough for a cart. Two hundred yards farther we finally saw the brook. The forest suddenly opened up, and below the bluff a tiny green field glowed in the sun. Under the sloping bank the brook splashed over boulders and among rocks. The woods rose lush on both sides, but across the way the water had made a wide bed and left a hard-packed bank on which to walk. We walked upstream. Then we heard another roar.

The banks narrowed, there was less daylight here, and, after every few steps, we had to cross the brook. In an elbow, the wild boars had dug a mud bath in the bed. Their hoof marks were everywhere, and mud was splattered onto rocks, tree trunks, and overhanging foliage where they shook themselves, or fought, or—who knows—maybe danced.

The brook widened. We took off our shoes and waded. The roar grew. We were deep in the throat of the canyon. Our feet were freezing by the time we rounded the last bend and it fell into our sight.

On both sides, cliffs rose darkly to the sky. A few twisted plants had made footholds in their crags, but the rest of the stone was grey and hard against the green. And between the cliffs, from a cleft cut by a million years of running water, a white ribbon of water shot over the ledge and splattered into a wide, green pool down below.

We sat on a rock in silence.

~

So whether it is the waterfall, or the silence above the terraces, or the smell of broom in flower on the slopes, that small vineyard is still my favorite. Or maybe it's the entrancing perfume of the wine, spices that keep you inhaling to the end, a Syrah so lush and dark and rich that the brooding flavors go straight to the soul.

This is the one vineyard I prune by myself. I go early to catch the sunrise and watch it throw long shadows on the ground between the vines. In the morning there's often frost on the lower terraces, and the shears feel like ice between my fingers. But with the walls holding the heat of the sun, this is the first vineyard to flower, to arrive at véraison, the appearance of colors, and to mature; it is first into the cellar.

In the summer I pass weekly, freeing clusters around wires, thinning the grapes, and matching the load to the foliage of each plant so they mature evenly at least in each row. Then, starting in late August, I come twice a week with a refractometer, an instrument the size of a pen that measures the sugar content of the grapes, writing it down row by row, waiting until the last moment, the perfect time to pick. With the curve in the hill and the difference in heat between the low terrace and the high, we often have to pick the grapes as much as a week apart. But it's always the Syrah's fragrance in the vats that tells us that Tuscany's best season has begun.

25 ~ THE HEART
OF THE HOUSE

We had mountains of used terracotta tiles awaiting rebirth. I had to match them all by size; Fosco threatened to quit if I didn't. He'd already quit a hundred times, over the twisted beams, over leaving the windows different sizes, over forcing him to build walls around the doors, and of course over the double-mortaring around the stones. But this time he swore he would leave that second unless the tiles were the same size for each room, because he would lose what was left of his mind trying to lay tiles of different widths and lengths. That was when Piccardi sent the cavalry to the rescue.

The cavalry rode up in a cloud of dust on a motorcycle that seemed straight from a 1920s movie. When he got off and walked toward me, the dust cloud followed him as if it were his own personal storm. He was still a good distance off when he roared out in a voice that made me tremble, "*Sono* Vasco! *Mi ha mandato* Piccardi!"

Vasco was near fifty, all nerves and muscle, and his

voice was no accident; he had trained it in the army. He had been a sergeant, and though he retired years before, he kept his booming voice and loved to use it. Unknown to me, Piccardi had sent for him when he saw our Everest of tiles. Il Sergente, as he was called by all from that day on, would sort, organize, chip, scrub and allocate every tile to its predestined room, its proper place.

While Il Sergente worked happily, singing out back, Fosco and I were slowly going crazy in the old-sheep-pen-now-kitchen, trying to figure out how to put a three-foot-deep fireplace into a two-foot-thick stone wall, a wall which, among other things, was three stories tall and held up the whole house.

To understand how vital this problem is, one must know that, for Tuscans, the heart of the house has always been the kitchen. You cook there, you eat there, you gossip, read and sew there, you play cards there, you were probably conceived there, and, until not long ago, on blizzard-chilled winter nights, you slept there with the whole family because its fireplace was the only source of heat for the house.

As late as the Second World War, the fireplace in the kitchen and the small brick stove beside it—which held hot coals—was the only means of cooking. When I asked Nonna once how Tuscans ever decided that the best sauces, roasts, and stewed meats were those left to cook slowly for hours, she just laughed and finally said, "we cooked slowly because we had no way to cook fast."

Whether that was facetious or not, I don't know, but slow cooking is as much a part of the Tuscan soul as swearing. If you take those away, you might as well take the air, because breathing would no longer be worth the bother. Hence most new houses, apartments included, have as their indispensable feature a small fireplace in the kitchen. We had one at La Marinaia that was lit from September until April. The few times the fire went out during those months, the kitchen felt as if it had lost its life.

Il Colombaio was going to have a fireplace in the kitchen, even if the bloody tower was going to bury us alive as we built it.

The question was, how do you hold up the tower while you sledgehammer the bottom out from under it? Then one day at Trattoria Sciame, I had an extra grappa after lunch and, abracadabra, just as fast and clear as the Ten Commandments came to Moses, the God of Grappa sent The Fireplace Plan to me. When I relayed it to Fosco, he reacted in a way I'd never seen before. He turned away, held his head with both hands, snorted, and then laughed uproariously. Then he turned back to me, suddenly serious, and said, "*Madonna gonfiata*, it might just work."

On the other side of the wall we were about to destroy was the entranceway. So, on the entrance side, head-height, we dug a long, 4-inch deep, horizontal trench and inserted a steel I-beam. We welded two verticals to it (like a goal post) and put another horizontal on the ground to spread the load of the three-story tower. This, I thought, would hold up the wall while we excavated the kitchen side and built an arch to hold up the stones over the fireplace hole.

With the steel beams in place, we went back into the kitchen and began, most gingerly, to dig. And pray. We dug and pulled the stones out as tenderly as if the wall were made of eggs. They came one by one. Pouring sweat, we were almost at the end when suddenly there was a deafening crack above.

We ran like rats.

We stood out in the courtyard, our hearts in our throats. The tower seemed to have sagged but still stood. Then came the second horrendous crack, even louder than the first. From the upstairs window, Asea leaned out smiling and threw down two splintered boards he had just broken in half. We glared at him. His smile faded. "For the fire," he pleaded. "It's lunchtime."

Fosco turned beet red. I'd never heard him yell more than a single word before—my name—but this time he ran up the stairs laughing and yelling, "That's it! This time your *coglioni* are coming off!"

26 ~ IT'S RAINING DEER

The ten acres in front of the house stood full of dry twigs in tidy little rows. The problem was that it was already May and hot and getting hotter. The only way to avoid Death Valley was to water. There were two solutions: one was to put a tank behind the tractor with a short hose attached, drive slowly, and drench each twig with at least a gallon. But driving back and forth and standing around while the tank filled would be horribly time consuming, so we opted for number two: duct the water down and water with a long hose.

We ran a pipe from the cistern along the top of the vineyard, and at every fifty feet we installed a tap where we could simply attach a hose, drag it down the row, water one side, and then water the other side as we dragged it back. What a coup: quiet, relaxing, standing in the sunshine in beautiful Tuscany, enjoying the view, with a hose dangling effortlessly from your hand. I was in heaven. At least for the first half a day, after which there would be another week to go. Then, if the heat stayed and it still didn't rain, I'd have to start all over. By the tenth day I dragged that hose behind me like a ball and chain. And I started talking to God.

I prayed for a day of rain, or a few hours of rain, or even a passing downpour. Twenty bloody minutes! But my prayers were never answered, or if they were, the answer was "No!"

So I scaled back on what I prayed for: I'd settle for a stroke. Or a minor, but lengthy, earthquake to open the ground just wide enough to swallow every vine.

~

I felt like a Bedouin, condemned to the Sahara for eternity. Except Bedouins don't waste their lives standing in the bludgeoning sun, trickling drabs of water from a hose onto dead twigs. I trickled for days, for weeks, until I could no longer remember my life before tricking. I trickled humming, I trickled praying, I trickled in silence, and I trickled in agony. After three weeks, the dead twigs looked deader than before.

Then finally one night, with the water in the cistern gone and my hope almost dried up, it came. It started long after midnight with a breath of cool air, wafting like a ghost, through the open windows. It kept getting cooler until I had to pull the blanket over me. Funny how you almost never recognize the sound, thinking it's a cat on the roof tiles, or a lizard in the *coppe*r gutter. Plunk. Then it plunk-plunks again, and blends with the wind rustling the trees, louder until it blows and rains as if to carry the house away. I got up to close the window but didn't. I just stood and listened to the water gushing onto our vines.

In the morning, the vineyards were mud, and puddles shone like mirrors in the sun. Before the week was out, everything had changed. You had to look closely, but if you bent down far enough, the dead twigs showed a hint of green: the glowing, minuscule leaves of a live vineyard.

Deer eat anything green. They ate our lilac bush, lettuce, carrot tops, and one of my slippers. But what they loved more than anything else were the young leaves of tender vines. Especially ours, as if ours were somehow better than the other million bloody vines in the valley. Now, all you deer-huggers will say, "leaves schmeaves. What's a couple of bites of green?" Which were the very words I uttered in the spring. But when, through the summer, they began to strip the green off an entire vineyard more effectively than napalm— meaning that not a single grape would grow on those vines and we'd lose about a thousand bottles of Brunello di Montalcino in our first year of production—then you will understand why my attitude changed from "leaves schmeaves" to "I'll choke the bastards by hand."

However, I chose a more humane course: I built a fence.

We are not talking about fencing in a carrot patch. These are seventy acres whose property line looks like the seismogram of an earthquake. It runs through woods and gulches and cliffs. So the decision to fence didn't come easily, although it did come with a gift.

One of the democratizing laws of Tuscany is that you can hunt on *anyone's* property. This may sound ideal, as some poor, propertyless soul can go maim and slaughter just like a millionaire. The downside is that the son of a bitch, often from as far as Rome, chooses to do his maiming and slaughtering right under my bedroom window at six o'clock on Sunday morning. But once you fence in your property, and register it in the *catasto*, you must, *by law,* put small metal signs every two hundred feet that say, "Land closed. No hunting."

Of course it broke my heart to do this to my redneck, gun-toting co-patriots, but then, as they say, "The law is the law."

The plan was to put up a simple sheep fence, which does not look out of place in the countryside, just high enough to discourage the deer. But to make sure the deer went out and stayed out, I turned to infallible deer psychology. We fenced in three sides of the land, leaving the fourth wide open, for now, assuming that the deer would, within a few days, realize that they were fenced in, choose freedom, and leave peacefully through the fourth, open side. When, after three weeks, my deer-intuition told me they'd had enough, we closed in the fourth side.

There was a wonderful silence around the house. The hunters stayed outside the fence and their guns now went *pop* somewhere in the distance. The other good news was that the deer never jumped the fence. The *bad* news was that every silence-loving, vine-chomping bastard of them remained *inside!* And not only that. Judging by the hoof-marks that grew like smallpox on the ground, they had invited in every deer in all of Tuscany.

Time for Plan B.

Anyone who has ever seen Bambi's big ears perk up at the slightest sound knows that those appendages help the deer locate danger. In short, they run from noise. So I invited friends and neighbors in for a noise-party. They brought drums, horns, pots, pans, a trumpet, and guns, and a music teacher even brought a handheld xylophone. I myself brought the most ear-shattering noise of all: Tina Turner hollering from three boom boxes.

We spread out in a long line within sight of each other and began our noise march up the property. We yelled, clanged, blew, and banged. We could see the deer run for their lives across the vineyards and through the woods. But we were relentless; we kept on. And in the last big vineyard, as we closed in on the fence, I gave the signal and on a count of three, we turned on the boom boxes and unleashed our mortal blow: Tina.

Strategically placed and turned way past red line, the boom boxes blasted and Tina sang "You Ain't Woman Enough to Take My Man" at her most hair-raising, atom-splitting best.

Better safe than sorry, I left one of the boom boxes up there overnight, with a thirty-second shriek-loop blasting on repeat.

In the morning, I walked up to get it. Silence. The batteries were dead. The woods were still. Not a leaf stirred. No deer in sight. I walked contented through the upper-most vineyard, reached down for the box, and then I saw it. All around the box, as far as the eye could see, the soft, wet clay was patterned with hoofprints. I couldn't breathe. How could I have known? Who could have guessed?

Deer love to boogie.

Our little leaves grew into shoots. We had to plant the columns to hold the wires to which we'd clip the *palette*, little poles. This job was consigned to an outside expert. It's simple: you bring in a small excavator, put a column beside every sixth vine, and, with the bucket of the machine, gently push the column down.

They finished four acres in four days and you have never seen such a mess in all your life. The columns leaned in every direction, some were out of line, some were too high, and others were so low the stretched wire would simply pass above them. I had to call in Giancarlo and Il Sergente. Armed with a pick, a short stepladder, and a giant sledgehammer, they went to work, straightening, leveling, hammering, and sometimes pulling the column right out of the ground, filling the hole and planting it again.

Now came the wires. The lowest one would hold the cordon, the bent stem of the vine. From it, five or six shoots would sprout and grow upward. To keep these from flopping into the aisles we used a pair of movable wires that start on a lower hook and, and as the shoots grow, get moved up higher. At the top of the pole is another fixed wire. Ideally, for the wire to last and to avoid stretching, one would use stainless steel. But, because it doesn't oxidize, stainless steel shines forever.

"The last thing you want," Fabrizio explained, "is to have fifteen miles of blinding, glittering cobwebs in front of your house."

I could have named a several other "last things" I wanted, but I kept my mouth shut and settled for nice, dull, galvanized wire—which, unlike stainless, stretches, so I'll have to tighten it annually until the day I die.

While the vineyard in front of the house bloomed and thrived, Rino and I began readying the big, bowl-shaped vineyard near the spring. Here it was not just a question of tooth-and-plow loosening and turning the soil. The bowl was not perfectly regular—there were large dips and mounds plus a ridge crossing it—so we had major earth-moving to perform.

But Fabrizio couldn't just let us have fun pushing mountains around. He had to be scientific; it had to be perfect. If we only cut off the mounds and filled the dips, we'd wind up with some areas having ten feet of topsoil and others just bare rock. So, first we scraped the topsoil with enormous machinery and piled it high. Then we shaped the land, cutting and filling, and finally we put an even layer of topsoil back over it all. The final result was an almost perfect amphitheater, with ideal slope and drainage. There was only one problem: it was full of enough rock to build a house.

So now we had to drill, then destroy our perfect theater to bury the broken rock in drainage shafts below. The last task was for Rino and his excavator to turn over every cubic inch of soil to a depth of three feet and remove what rocks remained. If you know of a quicker way to bankruptcy, please let potential vintners know—it will save them much grief and time.

27 ~ THE ANCIENT CITY

*I*n the final phases of house restoration, nearly every day brought an unexpected present, something new to please the eye. A little elf of a man named Enzo came to oil all the beams and *correnti*, and within a few days they became rich-looking and dark, full of grain and swirling knots, as if they had been there since the beginning of time. He was to start painting the inside walls, but we first had to solve a minor catastrophe: the corners around the doors and windows that the masons had just spent a week making perfect, I wanted demolished and redone.

I had been in New York that week, but before I left, I made a drawing in the dust of how I wanted to have the plastered corners around all the openings rounded—"radiused" is the term used in architecture. The screw-up was on account of relativity—for while my idea of a rounded edge was actually round, say, like the curve of a wine bottle, to others (without naming names) it seemed to mean a corner sharp enough to shave with.

That was when, just before losing my mind, I found the Etruscan city.

It was the first time in the whole year I really lost my patience. I called over Fosco, picked up a rasp, went to the nearest window, and, with the calm of Buddha, rasped away their glittering razor edge down to wine bottle round. While I rasped, I explained, in a low voice, that it was silly, wasn't it, to restore a seven hundred year old house to original state, where the hand of man can be seen on every irregular piece, only to have all the corners look as if they had just been cut by a laser-guided saw. So why don't we, just for the fun of it, rasp down all the square corners and then re-plaster them, this time smoothing, by hand? I know it will cost more, but when you're going to the poorhouse anyway, what difference does it make if you arrive a day early?

Then I smiled, handed him the rasp, and walked out to the toolshed. I picked up the *pennata* and went way up into the forest, swearing in three languages. I began to hack and slash in fury, determined to go on until I'd clear-cut the planet. But I didn't get far. Within half an hour of hacking, I found, in the darkest part of the entangled woods, the first houses of what turned out to be a three-thousand-year-old city.

As I mentioned before, our property includes two hills. The locals called the first one *bollicina* or bubble, because it's so perfectly round. I noticed while working with Rino on the terraces below the bollicina, that it did not rise naturally out of the hillside, but was surrounded by a twenty-foot-wide, perfectly flat and obviously hand-leveled, ribbon of land. The sides of the bubble were artificially steep as if it had once been a tall, sheer wall like a fortress whose stones had fallen and been grown over. Like the Troy I didn't find around the buried urn.

As I hacked, I uncovered a knee-high wall whose stones had been placed with as much care as Machu Picchu. The wall was three feet thick and finished on both sides. Just six feet away and parallel to it was another wall of the same construction and height. I hacked through the woods to follow them. They dipped and climbed, always together, always parallel as if they had been guides for horse-drawn chariots, or perhaps a road protected on both sides. The walls ran into a flat clearing that, with the help of a retaining wall, was absolutely level. It was the size of half a football field: no one in his right mind would level this much land by hand for any use other than to build houses for people, because grains and vines grow just fine on slopes, and animals too can live well on hillsides. I took to the road again. Farther up, a ring of stone protruded from the outside wall. It sank deep like a well, but it also rose like the base of a tower. I scraped at the loam below it. Bits of ancient terracotta popped up everywhere.

I climbed the second hill. Here the double-walled road ended in a tight opening that could have been a gate.

Remains of stone walls, sometimes close together like a group of houses with adjoining rooms, sometimes isolated, dotted the forest.

The remnants of a rambling building covered the hill-top. Rooms opened into rooms that ran right to a cliff. When I hacked farther I understood why. We were less than fifty yards from the spring.

That night the family turned into starry-eyed archeologists in search of fame and glory. We hauled out every book we had on the Etruscans, even postcards from Chiusi where we'd seen their painted tombs. We washed the broken pieces I had found and spread them out on the table for a better look.

Some pieces were thin and curved—they must have been small bowls or urns—but most were chunks of ancient *tegole*, the flat roof tiles with turned-up sides, like the ones on Il Colombaio. But they weren't like *tegole* I had seen before; both the bottom and the turned-up sides were twice as thick as ours. And they seemed strangely pitted with dark spots inside. We washed and scrubbed but the dark spots—small holes—remained. And yet despite their bulk, they were strangely light. Then we looked closely at the drawings of Etruscan temples. They were the same shape as the Greeks', who had colonized these lands, but built on a smaller scale. The *tegole* in the drawing were enormous, four times as large as Il Colombaio's. So a temple tile's size would explain its necessary thickness, but what about the light weight? And the little holes?

For the rest of the week we did research every evening, but none of the books mentioned specific weight. Almost a month later, as I worked in the vineyard near the church, two pretty young women approached and asked if I minded their collecting pieces of terracotta from our land. I told them they could take everything but our roof. They were professors from the University of Florence doing research on an old Roman town, which had been a center for commercial grape-growing two thousand years before. Judging by pieces of tile they found—known to be used to conduct steam under the floors of Roman baths—the town was spread over Gaja's land and ours.

I mentioned to them, without saying where, the strange bits of *tegole* I'd found. Their eyes lit up. "Etruscan," they said almost in unison. They explained that the Etruscans' kilns weren't as perfect as the Romans'; the heat was less controlled, uneven, so their thicker pieces tended to warp. To compensate, they would mix straw into the clay. When the straw reached its flashpoint from the heat around it, it burned, generating new heat deep inside. This would warm the clay, bringing it closer to the temperature of the surface, thus lessening the warps. I could see now, on close inspection, that the small dark holes had the shape of bits of straw.

That weekend we dug. Forgetting poor Il Colombaio and the

vines, we were now Raiders of the Lost Rocks.

We found a lot of broken building tiles, but we also unearthed delicate bits that only a well-trained potter could have thrown. These were not the remains of shepherds' huts spread over our hills, from country bumpkins eking out a living. With temples and fine pottery, this must have been a city.

"There's only one thing missing," Candace said, drenched in sweat from digging. "If this was once a city, where are all the stones?"

I was ready for that. "Come," I said.

We scrambled out of the woods. Once we passed the trees, I told her to look down. Below us was Gaja's church with its odd tower, and around it stone buildings spreading like arms. Across the way, beyond a dip, stood Castelli's castle. Not long ago, a hundred people lived among its rambling walls, all stone and all downhill from our old city.

"Why," I said, "would anyone bother to dig up stones and shape and cut them square, when a few hundred yards away were the best-cut stones of all?" I said.

"Hm," Candace said. "I guess you can't be wrong all the time."

28 ~ TRACTOR WILD

*P*lanting a vineyard to make your own wine is not for those with short attention spans. Clearing a field of stones and tilling it takes a summer, letting the ground settle takes until the spring, planting and watering takes the enamel off your teeth, and harvesting your first high-quality grapes takes three years. But there are some pleasant stops along the way.

The first is in late June of the second year, when you look at your vines and swear you've gone mad. Until now you've had only lifeless, brown earth, then, for a few months, only lifeless brown sticks, then, for a year, fields of lovely green, and now, all of a sudden, without a word of warning, you begin to see purple spots before your eyes. Grapes. Maturing grapes.

I got so involved with the details of how to tie vines, and hoe around each stem so the stronger weeds wouldn't choke off the weaker vine roots, and run a tractor without destroying house and surroundings, that the changing color of the grapes had completely escaped me. But right after the moment of joy came days of full-blown panic: What do we do now?

I had just finished mastering the little tractor with caterpillar tracks and was gloating at my success. It had not been easy. We have two tractors. One is expensive, German, with a cabin and air conditioning, which is driven with a steering wheel, like a car. Then there's the little, open one with caterpillar tracks, that we use for hard work like ploughing, tilling and hauling, which has, instead of a gas pedal and steering wheel, levers. Lots of levers. Enough to drive someone much more stable than I out of his mind. Now I know you have about as much interest in how a crawler tractor works as you have in the digestive system of a Madagascar fruit bat, but I'm going to tell you anyway.

First off, the tractor is a Fiat, made in Italy, meaning years have been spent engineering it to be as complicated and uncomfortable as possible. For example: it is only 24 inches wide not counting the tracks. So the first thing you realize as you get in it is that you might never be able to get out. Your second realization, as you sit there in a position normally reserved for women giving birth, is that it has more levers than all the slot machines in Vegas.

First, you choose one of eight speeds using one of two levers. Then you choose forward or reverse with another lever. Give it some gas, not with a pedal, but with—you guessed it—a lever! But, does it work like a gas pedal on a car, where to go faster you push, and to go slower you release?

Hell, no! That would be common sense. To go faster, you pull, and to brake you push with all your might. To get the damned thing moving, you have to engage the clutch (but not the clutch *pedal,* the clutch *lever*). To steer the tractor— hold on to your hat—you step on a foot brake: left foot brake to turn left, right foot brake to turn right. To make small adjustments you have to manipulate yet *another lever.* To turn real hard, you engage one of *two* other long levers. And to raise or lower the basket you pull another lever. In case you've lost count, you have so far engaged four hundred and ninety- seven levers. This is only a medium-sized challenge if you're plowing, let's say, a wheat field in Kansas where the nearest vertical impediment is a four-inch-tall gopher sixty miles away, but it's a whole other story in a 70-inch-wide alley of wood columns and wire.

But I'm no fool. I didn't just leap into that jungle of levers in the middle of a vineyard and started yanking. No sir. First, I practiced in a small field, bare but for a few trees, some shrubs, an old stone wall, a chicken coop, and a fence.

I got on, turned the key, and the engine sputtered. I went to give it gas so it didn't stall, pulled the right lever but in the wrong direction—bam. Stalled. I started over and went to pick a gear. The two gear levers of the Fiat are made to get a laugh: aside from some numbers, one has a drawing of a turtle, the other of a bunny. No male with a drop of testosterone left in his body would ever pick the turtle. I picked the bunny and the number 4—my lucky number— then started to pull the accelerator lever while I slipped in the clutch lever, and the engine roared. The tractor surged and did a wheelie—which is impressive, considering it has no wheels—then it took off like a bat out of hell, right for the chicken coop. I calmly yanked eleven levers, and after only a little bucking and three donuts I had her serene and docile, running at just a hair over fifty miles an hour straight at the old stone wall.

This wasn't the time to pick and choose a lever so I pulled back *all* the levers as far as they would go. But the Fiat was no horse. Instead of slowing as I'd hoped it would, it sped up, running in the same overall direction but with the added attraction of doing so in slalom, to the profound disappointment of a handful of small shrubs, which had been counting on a somewhat longer life. Inches from the stone wall I remembered the footbrakes. I jammed on the left—my lucky foot—and the beast spun away, free from calamity, but pulling seven G's so all the blood in my body ran into my left knee. When I regained consciousness we were mowing down some trees. That was when I remembered that I actually like turtles, but there was no time for musings, for the chicken coop now loomed dead ahead. I tried a lever I hadn't tried before, which resulted in lowering the plow, so we no longer merely mowed down the trees ahead, but also churned up the ground right behind.

The chicken coop was a breeze. It was made of soft sandstone blocks, so I had no problem converting it to a much-needed pile of sand. The fence gave me some trouble. It was of chicken wire, which, with a bit of swerving, I managed to avoid until the last minute when one of the tracks nicked a single link, at which point the fence rose *en masse* and, in five seconds, wound itself completely around the track.

Candace stood on the sidelines with her arms crossed, surveying the field. "Finally, we can plant some alfalfa," she said.

29 ~ TRIP TO BORDEAUX

With our first Tuscan grape harvest staring us in the face—requiring lengthy preparation and mountains of special gear—we did the only logical thing under the circumstances: we drove to Bordeaux. This was no frivolous escape, because between St. Emilion and the Haut-Médoc are made some of the world's greatest wines: Petrus, Cheval Blanc, Château Palmer, and Château Margaux. This was a spy mission. If you are going to steal ideas, you might as well steal from the best.

Fabrizio, with some excellent contacts in Bordeaux, had a friend put his hunting lodge just west of town at our disposal for a week. During the day we scoured vineyards and wineries, and in the evenings we worked hard cementing our arteries with *foie gras chaud en feuille de choux* (warm goose liver in cabbage leaves), *confit de canard*, chicken with crayfish, young goat with garlic, and watercress and chicken liver salad, followed by a small pickup truck full of cheeses, and lastly *tartes et gâteaux*, all the while taxing our livers with bottles of *deuxième crus*.

Winemakers seem to have an instant bond between them, much like the secret society of the Masons. Their eyes light up and hearts open upon encountering a fellow eccentric. The hospitality at the wineries, especially the small, family-owned ones like ours, seemed to know no bounds. Whole mornings were spent tasting wines—some vintages decades old—then we were invited for lunch and given nut-by-bolt tours of the equipment used in vineyards, from magical plows that go in and out between vines, to spinning drums used to remove the stems just before fermentation, to the peristaltic pumps that don't pound the wine like the piston types.

In the fermentation sections of the wineries, we received lectures on the ideal shape and proportion of vats for maintaining the most skin contact; dissertations on the best way to keep the cap wet, whether it was pushing the cap—the thick mat of skins compacted above the liquid by rising carbon dioxide—down by hand, with a machine, or simply pumping the wine on top of it.

In the cellars, long discussions went on about whether to age in small oak barrels called *barriques*, where the wood has maximum contact with the wine, or in *tonneaux* twice as large, or in the traditional giant oak barrels.

Our first decision to make was about the vats, large open containers where the grapes would spend between twelve and twenty days fermenting. Some swore it best to ferment in big wood vats; others chose cement, where the temperature is constant; but most went for stainless steel. Not only was it more hygienic—nothing can ruin a wine quicker than unwanted bacteria—but the temperature of the must, a mixture of skin and liquid, could be controlled to perfection via built-in cooling jackets.

Our minds reeled from the condition that a friend once called The Tragedy of Choice. Until we entered the winery at Château Palmer.

Inside a vast, softly lit space were the most remarkable vats we'd seen so far. The three long rows of tall, stainless vats glittering before us were not the normal cylinder shapes we'd seen everywhere else; these were truncated cones rising toward the roof. Around each cone shone three raised bands of steel where cold or warm water ran to maintain temperature. The welding of the seams was as good as on any yacht, and the fittings of the doors, valves, and gauges—were all finished like jewels. It was love at first sight. I simply had to have them, even if it meant never eating *foie gras* again. I quickly copied the name of the maker from a bronze plaque above a valve.

The next morning we phoned the factory. It turned out they made enormous stainless steel storage tanks for trucks and warehouses. Unfortunately, the work they had done for Château Palmer had been a favor for a friend. I cajoled, I pleaded, I said I'd settle for three small ones for now, half the size of Palmer's, and I even thought of threatening, but I had forgotten how to do that in French. So I stuck to pleading. Then I finally remembered the fuel that France runs on:

snobbish pride. I mentioned that every vintner in Tuscany would die of envy with these jewel-like tanks in our cellars. Made in France. There was silence on the other end of the line.

"Can you wait until the spring?" the voice gently conceded.

I told him I could wait 'til Judgment Day, just as long as I could spend eternity with his vats.

It was a done deal. All we had to do was go home and measure our winery; they would fabricate three vats to perfectly fit our space.

I was in heaven. We took Sunday off to celebrate and drink a toast in the town of Margaux, next to the Château.

For a winemaker, Margaux is the equivalent of the Catholic's Lourdes. It was one of the few times in France that I was distracted from my meal. Out the window, the place was paved with vines; there wasn't a tree or flower on the horizon, and even the roads were kept narrow to make more space for planting. I have no memory of what I ate that day, but I do recall that right after lunch I jumped up and ran out into the vineyard. I hadn't suddenly and completely lost my mind, but all at once the place looked familiar; the width of the rows, the spacing of the vines. I measured with my 12-inch shoe. I was right. Both isles and space were precisely that of the vineyards we planted back home.

I strolled back to the table with a noticeable jump in my step.

If it was good enough for Château Margaux, it was

good enough for us.

~

Brains clogged with information and arteries with cholesterol, we headed home. We were so full, we thought we'd never eat again. But by late afternoon we were craving some of the Italian northwest coast's light seafood. Indeed, one of the grand joys of the trip from Montalcino to Bordeaux is the overnight stop at the tiny port town of Portofino. It is Europe's most beautiful—and for sailors, safest—small harbor. From Santa Margarita onward, the winding road is etched into the cliff just above turquoise waters. It ends suddenly at the foot of steep hills in what was, in those days, a quiet fishing village with a tight crescent-shaped harbor almost completely closed off to the sea.

Portofino is encircled by bluffs, with many-colored fishermen's houses wedged between them and the cove. Brightly painted fishing skiffs color the shore, some right side up, others upside down on the gentle shoal that forms the harbor's end. Fishermen fix their boats and mend nets strung on racks or piled in mounds along the seawall, their shouts and laughter bouncing between the houses and the bluffs.

To the south is a promontory with lush gardens and a church. If you can tear yourself away from the view you have sitting on the churchyard wall, you can hike on a path to a lighthouse three kilometers distant to watch the sunset. But the best show is in town. With the light of the setting sun bouncing off the clouds, the houses glow in colors as rich as dreams. The seawall swarms with everyone in town, sitting, walking, and gossiping as the last sailboat or fishing boat pulls in for the night.

Lights come on slowly in the houses, some fishermen light lanterns in their skiffs, and the reflections dance on the water. The voices fall with the darkness and hinges creak as shutters thud softly shut.

We ate dinner at an outdoor table set behind the skiffs lying on the shoals.

The world's best pesto is made here in Liguria. It's not just the flavor that I find so memorable but the way it is served: not on cut pasta, but on large sheets of lasagna. Whoever thought of flying in the face of *tagliatelle* or *fettuccine* or *maltagliate*, I don't know, but God bless them, for there is something festive in eating it with a fork and knife, next to the sea on a warm Mediterranean night. The second course is almost always fish. The Ligurians' favorite way to cook it is with olives. These are not the big, green olives of the south, or even the peppery small green ones of Tuscany. The olives here grow on steep, terraced hillsides, beaten by winds and scorched by sun, so they are tiny and black, with little flesh but much flavor, and baked alongside the fish they form the perfect culinary pairing. Merciful to our arteries, we skipped dessert that night, but we made up for it by honoring France with a glass of cognac.

With the family safely in bed, and the cognac aflame inside me, I went for a long walk around the sleeping town. There is a sense of mystery walking the streets of a foreign place, alone, after midnight. Perhaps it's the absolute silence, or it's that you are more aware of it when you're alone. Smells, thoughts, and views are all amplified. You fill in the dark shadows with your fancies or your dreams.

The port teemed with shadows. I circled the cove among skiffs below dark houses. Cats searched for discarded fish heads and jumped up to raid bait buckets in the rigging.

The moon came through the cypresses on the hill, and, as if caught in a wicked act, the cats cowered. I turned up a narrow alley to the churchyard. The town seemed a stage set and the night breeze from the hills enveloped me in the fragrance of rosemary and sage.

30 ~ THE MASONS' GOODBYE

*I*l Colombaio was alive again. Abandoned and left to crumble for a generation, her walls were now earthquake-proof; her roof could withstand the average asteroid; and her windows and doors, lovingly made by Scarpini, would keep out the strongest Tramontana winds in winter.

Pignattai's brother, Arnaldo, came to lay Mario's travertine tiles, now polished to a high sheen, and the old terracotta tiles, cleaned and neatly piled. He was silent and precise, a master at his work. His helper was chatty Occhialino—"little glasses"—as ironic a name as was brooding Gioia's, for Occhialino wore specs so thick one doubted he could see through them.

As calm and patient as Arnaldo was, Il Colombaio almost drove him mad. Unlike most *poderi*, which belonged to big estates with ample funds to hire real masons to build them, Il Colombaio had always been an independent friary inhabited by monks as poor as their mice. Their masonry skills were minimal, and desire for perfect structures seemed against their faith. In fact, judging by the bizarre angles where the walls met, they must have had added an eleventh commandment: Thou Shalt Not Square. And, by God, they stuck to it, for there wasn't a single right angle in the house. A dear philosopher friend once came to visit, and, looking at the untrue corners and bulging walls, exclaimed, "How metaphysical!"

Arnaldo was no metaphysician. He liked solids. And straight walls that joined perfectly square so he wouldn't have to cut every *testa di cazzo, maledetta puttana di quella Madonna spanata!* (translation censored) tile into rhomboids, trapezoids, parallelograms, and the shapes of various unspecified organs. With no right angles in the house, every room became the focus of lengthy discussion about where to begin laying tiles to compensate for the weird shapes, and what pattern to make with them; herringbone or staggered like bricks, or should we lay a border, or wouldn't it be quicker just to get a bulldozer and build the bloody house from the ground up again. But, more often than not, the work went on in silence; only once in a while would I hear a gurgling shout, then see a tile fly through the window and land at a record-breaking distance from the house. Day by day, the floors became so colorful that by the end, we were reluctant to put even the smallest carpet over them.

One morning came the blessed event. We were late, having

picked up the last door, a rare, ancient, two-winged treasure, its upper part made of heavy pieces of chestnut, like a trellis, each piece let into the one below. This, with a small roof over it, was to be the closure for the courtyard. I drove up to the house and my heart beat with delight.

There is a Tuscan saying that it is wonderful to see masons just twice in your life: the day they arrive and the day they leave. At the top of the drive was the masons' truck packed with the gear they had brought in, day by day, over the last eighteen months. My delight faded when I saw Fosco approaching. His face was drawn, his eyes looked away. Even Asea wasn't smiling.

Eighteen months is a long time, especially when you work together every day, building a house, piece by piece, which might stand for a thousand years. Handshakes turned into hugs and kisses on both cheeks. No one spoke. Only Buster came running down yelling *arrivederci,* not to them, but to Candace and me because he wanted to go and be a *muratore,* a mason, and work with Fosco.

The three of us stood silent as they disappeared down the road, leaving the dust to billow over the vineyard.

31 ～ AN ATTIC IN ROME

*T*o become a world-renowned winemaker, you must possess three things: an enormous passion for your vineyards and cellar; a perfectly trained nose; and the telephone number of the Suicide Hotline.

～

Having a passion for your vineyards and cellar doesn't just mean loving to own them; you need to love and care about each step along the way: from choosing the fields and planting the vines to looking after them day after day, season after season, from pruning in winter to maintenance in spring, through the long maturation, to the thrilling—and excruciating—autumn days of harvest.

When a Greek tycoon bought Château Margaux forty years ago, he hired Emile Peynaud, the world's foremost wine expert at the time, as a consultant. When he asked Peynaud to make the world's best wine, story has it that Peynaud replied, "that's easy. Just give me the world's best grapes."

To make the world's best grapes takes long days and a lot of sleepless nights. The winery and cellar work is just as demanding as the vineyard work, with an extra requisite thrown in—obsessive attention to detail and hygiene. Every step in the process—de-stemming, pumping over, *delestage,* pressing, racking—needs to be perfectly executed. Wine is alive, just as you and I are. If exposed to the wrong bacteria— even in the bottle—it gets sick. Left untreated, it might not die, but you can sure as hell kiss it goodbye.

Long before our first harvest, we asked Carlo Corino, wine consultant to big names like Frescobaldi, Gaja, and Planeta, to be our consultant. Utterly naïve, I asked him for the one secret of making an outstanding wine. He looked at me as if I had two heads, then he laughed out loud. "If I knew that," he said. "I'd be a billionaire. The truth is that there isn't one. There are a hundred. And they all have to be done perfectly, without fail."

~

A sensitive nose is a must. Not only does it allow you to smell the aromas and perfumes of wine in its various stages from fermentation vat to bottle, but much more important, it lets you sniff the *off* odors—an indication that something is about to go amiss—at their earliest stages, so you can effectively intervene with procedures like racking or fining to remove the source of the problem.

An untrained nose, however, can be easily deceived.

Short of a full university education as an enologist, the next best thing is a professional sommelier course. Not only does it instruct one in the process of making wine, but it also trains the nose to every conceivable odor in the cellar. It is a long commitment—normally two years of arduous study, and not to be confused with a wine-tasting evening at your local cheese shop.

Soon after we planted the vines, it became apparent that my nose, while a visually impressive aquiline beak, has the olfactory sophistication of a potato. Training it to smell a range of aromas would be as hopeless as teaching break-dancing to a slug.

Our ace-in-the-hole was Candace. She can smell a rose at twenty paces, a skunk from the next county, and the bouquet of our glass of Syrah from across the room. Not only does she know grand wines, but she has an artist's soul and a scientist's mind, and, just as importantly, she is a card-carrying wino. She was the perfect candidate for Italy's best sommelier course in Rome. As luck would have it, life would take us on a two year Roman holiday.

When Buster returned to school after a year of home schooling, he was instantly first in his class. But within three weeks, because of his irresistible urge to chat and play, he was headed for the bottom. We asked for a meeting with the principal to see what could be done.

I should add here that we have no TV at home. We're not Luddites—we have computers and DVDs of every classic film ever made—it's just that life is too short for channel surfing, and potatoes are best grown in fields, not on the couch. For real drama and entertainment, we seek out live people. Or we fight.

The principal was polite. He told us that the problem was Montalcino. Now a famous wine town, the school was no longer made up only of well-disciplined locals but also of a group of freewheeling *stanieri*, foreigners. We thought he meant the student from Tunisia, another from France, and ours from New York, but no, he exclaimed, they were fine. They were being influenced by the misbehaving *stranieri* who came to the school this year from Sant'Angelo.

Sant'Angelo is a town six miles away.

We paled.

Your son is a lovable child, the principal cooed, but he has to ignore the others and concentrate on his studies. We asked: do you have any special homework exercises? No. Any psychological training games? No. A psychologist? No. Any suggestions? The principal leaned back in his chair, blew a cloud of cigarette smoke in the air, and said with a heavy tone, "I think he should watch more TV."

That was Friday. On Monday morning, we had Buster enrolled in St. George's British School, a private school in Rome.

We needed an apartment in Rome to live in during the week. To remain consistent with the Máté lifestyle, it had to be cheap, weird and eminently impractical, which it turned out to be.

"It's a fifth-floor walkup," Maria the realtor said,

"between the river and the Spanish steps, in the oldest neighborhood, with stunning views all around." She said it was one of a kind. We walked across the town.

By then, Rome was mostly closed to cars, plus it was the Giubileo, Christ's 2,000th birthday party, so all the buildings, monuments, and bridges that for decades had a grey overcoat of soot, all of a sudden took on bright colors, and marble shone like the day it was hewn. We wound down narrow alleys, past Piazza Navona, the parliament, and the river, and ended on Via della Lupa, the street of the she-wolf, one hundred meters long.

"That's where Caravaggio used to come and pray," Maria said, pointing at a church. "And that's where he ate, and that's where he had his hair cut," she nodded at a barbershop on the corner.

With a key the size of a hammer she opened a tall wooden door, and we began to climb the worn marble stairs. The ceilings were unbelievably tall; each flight of stairs seemed endless. When we ran out of oxygen, we stopped.

"Fifth floor," Maria gasped.

I thought she'd reach for the door ahead, but instead she turned onto the bottom of yet another set of stairs. With no window, they led up into darkness.

"Your private stairs," she wheezed. Up and up we climbed. She opened the apartment door, and light poured out from a quaint entrance. One wall was all frescoes, another stained glass, and on the third—I swear to you—were more stairs. A dining room to the left opened into a living room with a real fireplace, and both had big glass doors that opened onto a broad terrace shaded by lush plants. We went out. Rome and the Tiber lay at our feet. Past a small kitchen was a study that opened onto another, smaller terrace overlooking Rome's domes and hills.

"Where do we sleep?" Candace politely asked.

Maria went back to the hall and opened a narrow door, which I had thought to be a closet, but lo and behold, what lay there? More stairs. The bedroom was an attic with windows on three sides. We looked at each other and knew this was it.

Two years later Candace was a certified sommelier in Rome.

32 ~ THE VIPER

*O*nce in a while someone enters your life and you wonder, "My God, how could I have lived so long without him?" Giancarlo was that someone. Considerate and kind, he is the most loyal of friends, and cheerful beyond all reason. His love for our vineyards, olives, and woods equals ours, but his concern for doing things right, and his attention to the slightest detail, be it building a footbridge, hoeing the artichoke garden, or making sure there was enough firewood for the winter, allowed me to go to sleep at night thinking, "everything will be alright. Giancarlo's here."

Once Alvaro, the Armageddon, and his death threat left for good, Giancarlo truly bloomed. We planted hundreds of rosemary and lavender bushes around the house, accenting them here and there with bigger shrubs of *corbezzolo* and *lentaggine*. The trees were growing well, the pines throwing shade, and the cypresses tall enough to sway in the wind. We planted a rose garden by the house entrance. Its colors flushed against the stone walls and green lawn, which we kept verdant all summer—a rarity in Tuscany—with water from Gioia's aquaduct.

As the tiny clusters of grapes appeared late one spring, I was passing through the vineyard, with Giancarlo and a couple of helpers, removing suckers—shoots without grapes—so they wouldn't rob the ones with grapes of nutrition. Quick-growing, the shoots were fragile—a light snap at the base sheared them—so it was a relaxing job that required little effort and no bending. The day was balmy and we gossiped as usual. Giancarlo recounted a joke at which he laughed so hard he could barely finish the punch line, but he stopped suddenly in mid laughter and said, "*Porca troia,*"—pig swine—"*una vipera.*"

He wasn't kidding. On the tractor path between the vineyard and the olives, gliding calmly through the dust, a viper made its way toward the house. Being a fanatic about keeping the place clean, I could find no stone or stick to kill it with, so I ran to the tool shed. When I came back with a shovel, the three of them were standing near the house by the roses, looking around at the hoed dirt at their feet. "Where's the viper?" I exclaimed.

"It came up here," one of the helpers said. "Then it went among the roses,"

"While I went to close the front door . . . " Giancarlo said.

"He must have gone in a hole," a helper said.

"There are no holes," the other said.

"You're the hole," Giancarlo said. Then he added softly, "Francesco, don't move. She's right next to your leg."

It was strange time for me to note that *vipera* is feminine in Italian, but then again I didn't have much else to do right then.

"Move your left leg toward me very slowly," Giancarlo whispered.

I did. Then I looked down. The viper was halfway up a rosebush, wound tight around its woody trunk.

"I'll kill it with the shovel," a helper offered.

"Like hell," Giancarlo said. "You'll just chop down the rosebush and she'll get away."

"Nobody move. Just keep an eye on it," I said. "I'll be back."

I ran to the green house and came back with shears. They were professional shears with aluminum handles and stainless blades as sharp as razors. I opened the blades, leaned down, and crept to the rosebush. Slowly, with barely perceptible moves, I reached toward the viper. It raised its head but stayed still. The blades shone near her and she opened her jaws to bite, but I was faster. The viper fell in four short pieces to the ground.

I heard a unanimous gasp and they looked at me in horror, as if a viper cut to bits was somehow worse than a whole one that could kill you.

~

In early September, the first rain fell since June. There had been a few thundershowers that had saved the grapes from shriveling and adding an unpleasant flavor of raisin to the wine, but this was the first rain that left puddles on the ground and made the dirt in the vineyards stick to our shoes.

Fabrizio had us run the tractor through the vineyards with a rake behind it to crumble the surface dirt so that it would act as a duvet, guarding the soil beneath from the blazing sun. So worked, the soil also absorbed every drop of rain. The next morning the grape leaves were noticeably fresher, and the day after that, they looked full again.

Giancarlo beamed as we worked in the woods that morning. "In ten days," he said, "you'll see a miracle at your feet." I immediately thought "viper," but no matter how I coaxed him, he would say no more.

⁓

We spent the week getting ready for *vendemmia*.

Most large modern vineyards harvest mechanically; a machine drives through and plucks the clusters, dropping them into a trough. Smaller vineyards pick by hand into plastic pails but then dump them into a big bin dragged behind a tractor. Neither method is ideal for top-quality wines, because when grapes are piled high—especially the optimally mature ones—their weight can crush and burst those on the bottom. The juice that comes out will begin to oxidize and turn acidic before the grapes reach the cantina.

So, per Carlo's instructions, we were to handpick into rigid plastic boxes, each holding thirty pounds. The boxes would go to the cellar on the tractor—we had a blacksmith create a little cart to fit our narrow rows—and the grapes in them would be poured directly into the destemmer, which sat on a pad outside the cellar window.

Every day I would pass through the vineyards with a refractometer. I was just finishing the top terrace of Syrah when I heard Candace's excited voice calling from above. "Chum! Chum! This is a miracle!"

~

Candace tends to stay calm under fire. A few years back, in the Gulf Islands of British Columbia, we were sailing our cutter through a dangerous, tight pass, where the currents can run at fifteen miles an hour and whirlpools form in seconds. Most sailors with detectable brain activity drop their sails, turn on their diesel engines, and motor through at slack tide when the currents are slow. But not I. The boat is called a sailboat and, by God, it was going to sail. So, into the pass we sailed, going with the current but against the wind. I was at the helm fighting the swelling eddies that tugged hard at the rudder while Candace was in the bow watching for rocks ahead. We were heeled with all sails flying and a smile on my face, almost halfway to a scruffy island, when Candace called calmly from ahead, "Chum, we should tack. I can see the bottom."

Seeing bottom is no big deal in the Caribbean or a South Sea lagoon, where the waters are so clear you can see your anchor dig in at forty feet, but in the North Pacific, where the plankton and algae thicken, you can only see the bottom when it's shallow enough to walk. If your boat has a six-foot keel like ours, seeing bottom means get out your rosary. At the helm, I had no view over the side, but being so far from the island, I could not imagine running hard aground. "We're just sailing over a shelf," I assured her.

"Chum," Candace chimed. "I can see a crab."

"Still ten feet," I snarled.

"I see the color of his eyes."

Then we hit. All sails flying, we stood like a statue in the middle of the pass.

I was fuming. Candace came calmly back, took off her hat, and sat down. "Might as well get a suntan if we're stopping for a rest."

"Why the hell didn't you say it was shallow?"

"I did. Three times."

"But without panic! Without emotion!"

She stopped spreading the suntan lotion and looked up. "Chum," she smiled. "Would that have made the water any deeper?" She lay back and closed her eyes.

So I knew that if Candace sounded excited, it had to be something big, and it was. Well over a pound.

If you walk out of our kitchen and turn uphill, you pass the garden, the greenhouse, and the old cistern, and end up on a path shaded by ilex trees. Cross a footbridge and you enter park-like woods full of ancient oaks with wild grasses growing at their feet. Where the oaks are sparse, pink wild roses grow, and among these now stood Candace and Giancarlo. Giancarlo was poking the rose bushes with a stick, and Candace stood under an oak, holding up with both hands something large and brown, as if making a solemn offering to the gods. It was a *porcino* as big as a plate. And that was just the beginning.

The field of oaks and roses is a good hundred yards long by about twenty wide. If you stop and look under the bent grass and search for a strange bulge under the matted leaves that fell the year before, you will see the dark brown heads of new *porcini* peeking out. Dozens of *porcini*, for this field had been known, as long as any native can recall, as a porcinaio, a *porcini* field. And year after year—as reliable as the swallows—the *porcini* return.

"Don't move, Chum. They're everywhere."

They were. You had to look for an empty spot to place your foot among them. We found sixteen, big and small, under just one tree. And in a spot where the roses thinned, there was something even better than *porcini*: a small patch of Caesar's favorite mushrooms, which the Tuscans call *ovuli* because, yellow and white, they look like open, hard-boiled eggs. Sliced thin and coated with lemon, they are one of life's splendid delicacies.

~

If Giancarlo is our guardian angel, Nunzi is his female counterpart. Small and energetic though she is over sixty, she helps Giancarlo in the vineyard and Candace in the wine cellar; she's my personal in-house psychologist, our window onto the valley gossip, but most of all she spoils us once a week with her cooking.

She prepares jams, bottles artichoke hearts, and makes pâtés, stewed rabbit, meat sauces, vegetable sauces, boar stew, stuffed veal and stuffed quail. That night, we ate *porcini*, stir-fried in olive oil and garlic, with a bit of parsley over freshly cut *fettuccini* that she had hand-rolled on our kitchen table that day. Her pasta melts in your mouth right down to your heart.

The next day, the Syrah reached 24 brix on my refractometer, and as complex a set of flavors as I could ask for. This was a grand moment. Three long years after we planted the flimsy-looking twigs, watered them, pruned and tied them, and worried about them day and night, it was finally time for our first harvest, our first real *vendemmia*.

33 ~ LA VENDEMMIA

*F*or the novice wine maker, the night before the *vendemmia* is a time to get blottoed, otherwise, you'll toss and turn, worrying if you filled the tractor with diesel and cleaned the grape pump with water or vice versa, or did you sharpen all the picking shears? Are the boxes turned over so they won't collect dew? Or did you call all ten pickers, and if you did, will they show up, or will it rain all day so it won't matter anyway?

All you can do is trust that your daily preparations for the past month have covered everything that Fabrizio, Carlo, and your common sense said to do.

We had no flashy winery that first year, not the big space with the stainless steel tanks that I dreamed of for next season. All we had was the old wine cellar under the house just big enough to ferment and age the first crop in oak barrels. Like the rest of the house, the cellar had been redone, and was spic and span, ready for the grapes.

This was the third year after planting; grapes of the first two harvests are too young to make into good wine, and even this year's crop we kept very low by drastic green pruning. Carlo suggested we try something difficult and time-consuming but which would yield a superb wine. He had us order fifteen oak *tonneaux* from France, but had the cooper ship the lids separately. This way we could ferment the must in the open barrels, then, once fermentation was over, a local cooper would close them up, and *voilà,* we could then pour the wine back into them through the bunghole and let it age two years. As a bonus, fermenting in wood would better integrate and soften the tannins, which, with young grapes, can be fairly harsh. It was genius.

The barrels were lined up, and the sparkling new stainless steel destemmer was outside the cellar window, ready to remove stalks and crush grapes just enough to break the skin. The most important thing I had to remember when filling the barrels was that as the yeasts boiled, they would create enough CO_2 to inflate a Zeppelin. The skins trap this CO_2 like little parachutes, and are pushed by the gas well above the liquid, where they become compressed into a layer as dense as bread dough. One should leave space for at least twenty percent expansion or the CO_2 will blow the cap right out of the barrel.

I awoke in nearly complete darkness. For an instant, I prayed for rain and a day of reprieve, but I quickly took it back and pleaded for a dry day, just enough to get the Syrah into the cellar. The grapes were ready. I picked up my clothes, tiptoed out so as not to wake Candace, and went out into the cold dawn. Worried but excited, I walked up though the ilex tunnel, past the sleeping *porcini*, and only when I started down the dirt path to the vineyard did I look down at my feet and my heart almost stopped. My shoes were soaked with dew. And if they were soaked, the grapes would be, too. I did not want grapes coated with water; I didn't wait weeks for the perfect ripeness just to have the must watered down.

I heard Giancarlo's little three-wheeler putt-putting up the tractor road, half an hour before starting time, as always. He looked at the grapes, then over at the sky.

"Don't worry," he said. "It's coming."

At first I thought he meant rain: the pickers would see it and stay home and I, their leader, could go back to bed and pull the covers over my head. But I was wrong. He pointed to the dawn-lit sky where red clouds raced toward us, blown by the Sirocco, the wind from Africa. Warm and dry, it would howl up the canyon, over the terraces, and through the vines, and for the small-berried, open-clustered Syrah, it would dry the dew in no time at all. By the time the sun came up, the Sirocco blew full force, but strangely it brought black clouds rolling over the hills.

The pickers began arriving. First were Nunzi and her husband Alfiero, by then in his seventies but still as upright as a pole, famous in the vineyards for his endless sex jokes. Then came Arnaldo and his niece Illaria, a twenty-four-year-old tomboy with an absurd sense of humor and wild spirit. They were followed by three retired pals from

Paganico—quiet, hard workers—then Federico, Gianni and last but never least, Vasco, Il Sergente.

The snapping of shears was drowned out by gossip as the baskets filled. We gathered them onto the tractor, then drove slowly to the cellar, so the grapes wouldn't bounce and crush each other. Candace was there ready to pump the must into the waiting barrels. We started the destemmer, a rotating drum with holes, whose rubber-coated blades separate the grapes from the stems. Candace started the pump. I peeked in through the cellar's open window, down into the gloom. She held the wide-mouthed tube over a barrel, and out oozed the crushed grapes. They came in a stream of blood-dark liquid, gushing in the dim light.

There was endless excitement in the vineyards. Giancarlo, more efficient than ever, was everywhere, picking, loading boxes, dispersing empty ones, all the while watching, like a kid, the fruits of his labor piled safely away. But he kept glancing at sky. The shears clicked faster, faces turning south where the clouds darkened, massing, full of rain; the red dust of the desert churned with the moist air of the sea. We had two more terraces to go. Candace came running from the cellar to help. We cut, stacked, loaded, and drove like mad through the smooth grass of the olive groves. Clouds now hung just above the pines. The wind strengthened and leaves flew. The first big drops fell and made craters in the dust. One terrace to go.

I ran for a tarp. Across the valley the castles vanished in the rain. As I burst out of the woods, the wind hit. It blew as if to clear the land of everything in its way. We covered the loaded crates with the tarp and lashed it down. The tractor was full, but still the pickers' shears clicked. We rushed for the cellar.

On our way back the rain started pelting, and that's when we saw them running, all the pickers each carrying the last full crates through the olive grove, bodies bent to protect the dry grapes from the rain.

After three days the yeasts in our Syrah came noticeably alive. If you put your ear to the barrel you could hear bubbling, and if you put your nose in it you'd gag on carbon dioxide. There was no cap formed yet, so we could still sleep in peace.

The Merlot was ready to pick a week later. The forecast called for a more dew overnight, which wouldn't necessarily damage the grapes, but without a breeze, we'd have to wait until noon for it to dry so we could pick. I was ready to battle the dew. We had three piles of vine shoots cut in winter, and by now they were as dry as straw and would catch fire in a flash. It is said that the heaviest dew falls just before dawn, so I set the alarm for three o'clock and went out, half awake, into the night. The air was still and heavy, perfect for dew. My teeth chattered from nerves and the cold. I lit the first pyre and it broke into a blaze, the sparks soaring into the darkness.

I had lit all three and was congratulating myself when I felt a stroke of cool air brush against my face. A breeze—a bloody breeze from the wrong direction. It was not strong enough to drive away the dew, but just enough to drive the heated air from our vineyards to those next door. A year of planning, and I got up that night to save Angelo Gaja's crop.

We did get the Merlot into the cellar that day, healthy but cool, so at least four days would pass before it began fermentation. The Syrah, on the other hand, was bubbling and hissing like a witch's cauldron.

~

At the end of September, after the Cabernet and Sangiovese had joined the Syrah and Merlot in the cellar, a long table was set in the old kitchen loaded with appetizers: artichoke hearts, olives, *prosciutto,* salamis, a goose neck stuffed and sliced, liver wrapped in bacon, and a mountain of varied *crostini.* Candace, Nunzi, and Ilaria were hard at work. The old domed oven belched heat, full of ribs, chickens, and pheasants roasting. Nunzi slipped in the platters of lasagna she'd prepared the night before. The hardened men who moved so fluidly and assuredly in the fields now shuffled awkwardly in the closed space, reaching hesitantly for food which, under the shade of a tree, they would grab and eat with gusto. Il Sargente gave orders and everybody sat down. I proposed a toast of thanks to everyone who had helped us, the glasses clicked, and everybody drank. Thunder cracked and fat drops knocked on the windows. Giancarlo toasted to "the one above" for waiting until we were done before sending the rain, and we all drank again.

Nunzi and Candace bustled in with two pots of *ravioli* afloat in still-steaming water. The *ravioli al carciofo*, with artichokes, had been made by Nunzi of a pasta so fine it had to be ladled with a holed spoon direct from the water onto plates; dumping them into a colander would have turned them into mush. We ate in silence, the *ravioli* melting in our mouths.

Lasagna with *porcini* followed—the pasta as fine as before—and it, too, vanished in silence as Tuscan dishes tend to do. The wine flowed and began to take hold, tongues loosened, and we toasted to the cooks. Alfiero toasted to the concerto for the deer, Il Sargente to the ten thousand hammer blows it took to plant the poles, Giancarlo to our aching backs from tying the vines, and then we toasted to the hail, the frost, and sliced vipers.

The smell of roast meats wafted through the house.

Nunzi roasted her homegrown chickens with their legs long from running around in her yard, veal stuffed with sausage and mushrooms, long ribs coated in olive oil and salt, and, at last, roast pork marinated and then cooked in shallots and Brunello.

Tuscan white beans from Candace's garden now steamed on the table, next to beet greens sautéed in oil and garlic. Our final treat was Nunzi's *tiramisù*, washed down with champagne.

We lit the fireplace at dusk, and while the fragrance of espresso and grappa filled the room we cleared the long table for the ancient game of Panforte. This is played with a flat fruit and nut cake as dense as lead, wrapped tightly in thick paper. There are two teams. One player at a time stands three steps from one end of the of the table and throws the *panforte* the table's full length, trying to get as close to the far edge as he can. Overhangs are best, but if you overshoot you're out.

There was strategy to consider: throw high and land hard or slide long and calculate friction? Several warmed up by loosening their arms, rolling their wrists. Alfiero, being oldest, advised the young. He leaned his long body forward in an arc, blinked hard to judge the distance, flicked his wrist, raised his arm, and, with a magnificently smooth and dramatic sweep, threw the *panforte* right under the table. We all burst into laughter.

"Bathroom break," Nunzi wheezed, "I'm about to lose it."

We remained silent as each player threw, and then exploded in gasps and shouts as the hard disc took flight then came to rest. When Nunzi stopped laughing she became surprisingly competitive, watching for feet crossing the line and measuring each millimeter after every throw. Giancarlo readied himself. The shy demeanor he wore around the vineyards was replaced by a concentration I had never before seen. He leaned and stretched so far he seemed to grow in height, and then with a slow, exaggerated motion, he threw. The disc flew. Like magic, the *panforte* landed on its edge and began a languid roll toward the far end of the table. But then, as if the devil got hold of it, it wobbled in an arc, changed direction, and now rolled right back to Giancarlo. With a loud thud, and to wild laughter, it landed at his feet.

It was time for intermission.

We toasted with grappa to the winners, the losers, the cooks, the *vendemmia*, the Sirocco, and the moon, but most of all we toasted to the barrels of crushed grapes now sleeping in the cellar.

I threw in the second half of the game, followed by Francesco, Buster, and Ilaria, all with unspectacular results. Then came La Signora, as Giancarlo steadfastly called Candace, who had until now stayed quiet in the shadows.

Candace seems frail. At five foot five, mostly legs, she weighs a hundred pounds when wet. She is, for lack of a better word, anti-competitive. She's been known to lose just to make others feel better, but she's lousy at it.

Twenty years before, she was in her first Canadian National Soaring Championship, a grueling nine-day competition among solo pilots flying one of man's most beautiful creations: 45-foot-wingspan fiberglass gliders so delicate and graceful, they make a racing sailboat look like a gravel barge. Sleek as an arrow and polished like jewels, with a tight cockpit under a plexiglas canopy, they have no engines but can fly enormous distances by getting lift from thermals—columns of rising air—to get as high as 20,000 feet. They then fly at 150 miles an hour to the next thermal, where they climb again.

Here at the foot of the Rocky Mountains, Candace was pitted against thirty veteran pilots, all male. She was young and pretty but most of them ignored her; they were there to race. They were there to win. The first morning, the course was laid out for the day: an exhausting two-hundred-mile triangle that would probably take five hours.

There was a tense quiet as thirty-one white planes gleamed on the runway. The tow planes lurched and pulled them, one by one, up to fifteen hundred feet, where the pilot released the towrope and went at it alone. Candace, her big racing number 5C burning in the sunlight, vanished in the sky.

Within minutes my radio crackled, "Five Charlie to Five Charlie Ground. My landing gear is stuck open I have to come back down." There was no choice; an open gear would slow her down tremendously in flight. She came back and we fixed it, but she was now last to fly. She didn't mind the late start time as she could stay out of the deadly gaggles of circling planes. The giant cones of rising air—like moderate tornados—lift the planes at over a thousand feet a minute, but are so narrow and tight that they all bank together, often wingtip to wingtip, to stay near the center in the strongest lift. Collisions were common.

Hours passed. A big storm was closing in. The ground

crews became nervous. Some began to hitch the trailers to the cars: there was little doubt the rain would come and destroy the wings' lift, forcing the planes down in some pasture, maybe a hundred miles from home.

The radios crackled; pilots told their crews to hook up. Some were giving last minute coordinates or descriptions of crossroads or barns near which they'd be landing. Some were so low they could describe the barnyard machinery. Then silence. They were down. Once down, or even at low altitude, the radios go out. Messages are relayed by those still in the sky. "Seven Yankee, ground, your pilot has landed safely." The whole sky grew black. In many major contests, pilots have died.

Curtains of rain came down in the hills. The radio crackled nonstop now, sending crews in every direction to try and find the downed planes, which the storm had scattered all over Alberta. The airfield was emptying of trailers and cars.

One of the pilots almost made it home. He had managed to weave and bob between the clouds. "Ten miles," he called, almost shouting with joy. Ten miles is close for a plane that can glide forty miles if it has a mile of height. Then not much later, "Five miles, still high," and we began to look for a small white spot in the now black sky. The radio stopped crackling. The rain hid the hills. Minutes passed with no plane in sight and no call. The pilot had hit a sinkhole, tried to land, but hit a ditch and demolished his plane just four miles from home.

From then on the radios fell silent. No word from anyone. No word from Five Charlie. That was the longest halfhour of my life. Ground crews are not supposed to call their pilots as there is only one frequency, and the pilots themselves might be trying to make their last desperate call. I envisioned everything: the plane in pieces, Candace in pain, dying alone. I got in the car turned on the ignition but to go where? North? East? South? Turning off the car, I stepped out into rain.

"Alpha Bravo Ground," the radio crackled, "your pilot has landed near the red silo at . . . " I didn't listen to the words, just the voice. Her thin, melodic, happy voice that rang warm and clear relaying the message, from somewhere in the dismal sky. After a pause, her voice rang out, as cheerful as before, "Five Charlie Ground, this is Five Charlie." She paused, then came a little sigh. "Still flying."

Thank God, I thought as rain poured down my face.

I might have done a dance. A quarter hour passed and the rain eased, but the sky was still dark as night and I became anxious again. I stared like an idiot at the east horizon. I saw white dots coming in through the darkness but blinked and they were gone. No call. I paced again and turned the squelch on the radio a dozen times to make sure it was working.

Suddenly a small white spot glowed on the blackened sky, a white spot that no blinking could wash out. It was far away, miles away, and low. Too low. Barely above a hill. It grew and I held my breath. Then the white spot sank against the dark-green of the ground. My heart raced. I stared.

The radio crackled with static.

Then the blessed little voice: "Five Charlie. One mile."

Her plane rose in the dark and her voice came again, anxious but laughing, "Jumping Jesus, I can't bring her down!"

She was so close I could see the airbrakes sticking up out of the wings, but even with the brakes out her plane was still rising. A monstrous, churning thermal was pulling Five Charlie up into the heavens.

"Okay," she sighed, "here I come."

She must have pushed her stick fully forward because her beautiful white bird, now vertical against the sky, was flying straight down, nose pointed at the ground. Pulling smoothly out, she did a sharp bank into the wind and forced the plane down, floating inches above the tarmac, then rolled to a rest before me. I tore open the canopy and hugged her tighter than ever before.

"Five Charlie, no miles," she smiled.

And then the rain poured down.

~

Now she was ready to throw her *panforte*. She did it with ease, without really trying. It slid and hung improbably, teetering on the edge. We gasped as it stopped. She'd won.

"Scusatemi," sorry, Five Charlie said.

~

As everyone got ready to leave, Candace vanished, only to return carrying a full pitcher. Then she went around and filled our empty glasses, telling us there was something we had forgotten to drink. She poured the thick, rubylike liquid, and a seductive cloud of perfumes swirled and filled the air. It reminded me of fragrances of tropical fruit in Burma, spices from the market in Marrakech, cinnamon from the high valleys of the Seychelles, the scent after a downpour in the Marquesas, singly and together, like banked clouds before a storm. We drank without a word.

Giancarlo, normally reticent, was first to break the silence. "I'm no expert," he said, "but I do know what I know. I've worked with a lot of wineries around here and this is by far the best must I have tasted."

Perhaps all of us sensed that something special was fermenting in the cellar. But not even I, the ultimate optimist, would have dared to guess that years later—after being nurtured by Candace through fermentation and aging for two years in oak *barriques*—that very same Syrah would be named number one of *Great Italian Reds* by Morrell's of New York, who called it a "true vinous gem."

34 ~ PURPLE VOLCANOES

*T*he Sangiovese grapes, in open barrels in the cellar, began their five-year voyage to becoming Brunello, and my hair began the five-year process of turning uniformly grey.

As I mentioned, precision at every step is the key to making unforgettable wine. The problem is to figure out just what the hell those steps *are*. The few comprehensive books on the subject are either completely impenetrable, or in sufferably dull. But Carlo saved us with his lucid and wise advice. In addition to working in the most famous wineries of Tuscany, he had also spent eight years in Australia, where his audacious attitude led to innovations and refinements.

That first year, he kept us to basic winemaking— grapes in wooden barrels. To allow for expansion during fermentation, he made me carefully measure and mark with chalk the line beyond which I must not fill the open barrels. But life does not always go according to plan. Or chalk lines. I filled the twelve barrels precisely to the line, but outside the cellar, the grapes were still being dumped into the destemmer, the pump kept pumping, and the grapes just kept gushing. I had two choices: the floor or the barrels. So I distributed what came as evenly as I could. The next few days we spent cleaning up, washing the pump, the destemmer, and the boxes, and putting away the gear and machines until next fall, while in the barrels the yeasts multiplied madly, on the verge of hard-core fermentation.

It was dark by the time we finished. Giancarlo, exhausted, bade me goodnight. I sat down on the steps of the cellar. Candace and Buster had were in Rome until the weekend, so I had the house, the cat and the worries to myself. Nunzi had filled the fridge with cooked meals so I would not starve, and I ate in the silent house, enjoying my solitude. I was rereading Conrad's *Heart of Darkness*, reveling in his sardonic humor and crystal-clear observation in the passage on sailing to Africa.

"We came upon a man of war anchored off the coast. There wasn't even a shed there, and she was shelling the bush. It appeared the French had one of their wars going on thereabouts. Her ensign dropped limp like a rag; the muzzles of the long six-inch guns stuck out all over the low hull . . . . In the empty immensity of earth, sky, and water, there she was, incomprehensible, firing into a continent. Pop, would go one of the six-inch guns; a small flame would dart and vanish, a little white smoke would disappear, a tiny projectile would give a feeble screech—and nothing happened. Nothing could happen. There was a touch of insanity in the proceeding."

I heard the cannon's roar. I thought, my God, this man can write; you live his story. I poured myself some fine plum brandy we picked up in Dordogne, then went off to bed.

Autumn is the most clement season in Tuscany. The heat eases, cool nights reign, and forest air tumbles through your windows, filling your room and lulling you to sleep. The only night-sound is the spring pouring from the clay pipe into the dark waters of the pond. I slept without dreaming until I heard the cannon roar again. The bloody French just wouldn't let up shelling. It took a while to realize I wasn't in Africa.

The cannon fired. I went to a window and listened. Hunting season hadn't yet begun and in any case, hunting wasn't permitted before dawn. I pulled on my jeans and went down to see if, perhaps, a log full of air pockets was exploding in the kitchen, but the fire was down; only two oak logs burned slowly on the coals. The cat looked startled. Kaboom. Suddenly I knew. I went out.

The night was clear; a fair breeze blew and brought the smell of the fire down from the roof. I opened the cellar door and stood back—even with the cellar window ajar, it is advisable to clear the air of carbon dioxide, which can knock you senseless before you realize it. I entered and turned on the light. Kaboom.

The barrels stood in perfect order as before, but what space I had left above the grapes was now filled with bloated, still-expanding mounds that rose purple and monstrous into the pale light. They hissed and gurgled and gushed like small volcanoes. The mounds kept rising well above the rims. They undulated slowly as if something menacing was writhing down below. They hissed in unison, and plumes of vapor drifted toward the ceiling. Then one mound quivered, cracked, and blew hoarsely as in anger. Far off in the shadows, another surged to new heights, and then it went, Kaboom!

Crushed grapes flew.

At first one glob at a time, then globs flew everywhere. Grapes hurtled like buckshot, like hail, like a gale-driven rain: at the ceiling, the walls, the windows, the door, and me.

My first impulse was to run and let the damned volcanoes fill the cellar to the ceiling, but the stubborn Hungarian in me took over and I grabbed the long stick we use to close the window. Charging like Don Quixote, I plunged the stick into the mounds, stirring to get the gasses out, to calm the explosive, hissing beasts. Once punctured, they belched, sighed and collapsed. I gazed around in victory. The cellar was a mess but nothing an hour of scooping and washing couldn't correct.

I was consoling myself with the thought that I had been lucky, for to be honest, it could have been worse—when it got worse. As if on a signal, the grapes counter-attacked. They surged in unison and the barrels overflowed. The purple masses climbed over the rims, teetered as if to tease me, and then suddenly spewed. More grapes oozed from the barrels than I remembered putting in.

With the stainless bucket I scooped the ooze by hand,

running from barrel to barrel like the man in the circus trying to keep a dozen spinning plates on teetering sticks. But it was no use. The more weight I took off the top, the easier it was for the gas to surface. I dashed to the storeroom for a hundred-gallon stainless vat and scooped full buckets from each barrel. I bailed without stopping, without thinking, barely looking, and breathing just enough to curse. The vat was full and I was drenched in sweat. The barrels stopped oozing. I sat down and took a deep breath.

I was always good at math; if I put the tractor in Rabbit 4 and pulled the gas lever as far as it would go, I could plough every grapevine out of the ground by sunrise.

35 ~ SANT'ANTIMO

*A*pproaching Montalcino from Buonconvento you climb until you come to a hairpin at the old gate of the town. From here a narrow valley winds east. In it is the estate of Biondi Santi, the family who invented Brunello in the 1800s; above it, vineyards rise to the Passo del Lume Spento, the Pass of Faded Light. A decade ago this was a valley of woods and pastures; a few sheep grazed and a woodcutter thinned the oaks, but the hand of man was a long-ago memory until wine lovers came and replaced the sheep with grapes.

In autumn, the valley now blazes reds and yellows in the evening light. At the valley's end sits the white travertine Abbey of Sant'Antimo, built by Charlemagne—Charles I, King of the Franks, Emperor of the West, Founder of the Holy Roman Empire. The story goes that on a pilgrimage to Rome in the late 700s he came upon this tranquil dale. The modest church he built still stands, but what takes your breath away is the vast and unadorned abbey, tall and austere.

Only high up on the corners do a few small gargoyles raise or twist their heads, but even they seem out of place—their marble is darker, the workmanship not the same—like fragments found and fitted from another age. At the crook of the nave an enormous cypress towers to the roof, standing like a stark black candle against the stone. A pasture spreads below the walls, with scattered gnarled olives, their trunks hollowed by beasts and weather through the centuries.

I was visiting a friend in Castelnuovo dell'Abate, a tiny, walled town perched on a hill nearby, and on the way home, decided to stop at the abbey for some quiet. It was dusk. The abbey glowed faintly as if it had somehow saved the sunlight of the day. It's a long walk on the dirt path to the door, long enough to leave the world behind.

I had been there often, at all hours of the day, but this was the first time that I noticed how the abbey, sitting alone at the far end of the flatland, has the forest rising a few steps from its door. And that is just it—the forest is at its door because the door faces the hill. The abbey has its back turned on the world.

Inside was no brighter than twilight. The interior is so simple it feels holy, with only an ancient wood crucifix and an altar. The light from windows above bathes the travertine walls and arches, saturating the stones. There was a gleam from a narrow side door, the door which in Tuscany, is reserved for the dead. An iron candelabra stood off to the right, its glowing candles melted stubs. I slipped into a pew below a pillar in the shadows. There were no sounds apart from pigeons cooing. Some time passed before I heard steps shuffling on the stone. A bell tolled.

A door to the side opened and monks filed in one by one, their heavy white cassocks whooshing on the ground, the rims of their hoods shadowing their faces. They bowed before the altar and then took their seats, three to the left and three to the right, facing each other in silent prayer. One began to chant, soft and effortless, but the sound filled the abbey.

They took turns chanting, clear, fearless voices ringing through the gloom. Then one of them swung an incense burner on a chain, its fragrance and the wafting smoke embracing the stones. They left as they had come, bowing to the altar, filing out through the door, one by one, white shadows in the night.

The candlewicks flickered in the liquid wax. I lit a fresh candle and it stuck out oddly high; it should have been unmistakable to all my beloved.

It's amazing how silent a stone house can be at night. I had lit the fireplaces the week before, one in the kitchen that would be kept burning until spring, the other upstairs in a small stove that belched heat like a dragon. Apart from the hissing flame, there was only the sound of our cat, Fiori, dreaming and purring under the kitchen table.

I turned out the lights and sat in the living room. I stared out through the arch into the moonlit courtyard and wondered, if I listened hard, would I hear echoes of the friars who had chanted here long ago?

36 ~ TASTERS FROM JAPAN

*T*he sunlit days of Tuscany can bewitch you: the cypresses pointing to the sky, the hard shadows, the cicadas, the long hot afternoons, the sunsets that set the edges of the clouds on fire. But it's the moonlit nights that steal your heart away.

Some of us are attracted to the darkness as a moth is drawn to the light. Perhaps it's my brooding Hungarian soul that finds itself at home there—just as it is thrilled by storms—or perhaps it's the sense that in the dark, something wondrous can happen.

Candace was never a fan of the dark. She said it was not from fear of man or beast, or even restless medieval ghosts, but that the dark was simply a place where nice people did not go. If any doubt about this judgment ever crossed her mind, it was set to rest one morning, once and for all, by Maria, a houseguest.

She was four years old and as high-strung as her mother, Giovanna, Candace's best friend since art school in New

York. They were staying in the guest room in the oldest wing of the house. Maria came down one morning, drowsy and tired, quite unlike her spirited self, and when asked what was wrong, she answered unblinkingly that she could not sleep because Signor Ladro, Mr. Thief, had walked around all night. For Candace, the case against the dark was closed, until late one moonlit night in the forest of Il Colombaio.

After our first year there, we invented a novel gift for Christmases and birthdays: paths. Candace started it one fall when she, Giancarlo, and Alfiero secretly recleared an ancient Etruscan path that crossed our impenetrable woods. A knee-high tunnel had been kept open by wild boar that ruled the forest in the night, but above it the growth was jungle. So the three of them hacked and cut and burned for days before they broke out of the woods at the bottom of the canyon into a small clearing by the brook. A sparse, wild grass grew in the open portion, but in the shadows, only moss. The sun could not reach here from November until March; the only light that penetrated was the cold light of the moon.

~

One evening, with Buster on a ski trip, Candace and I hosted two major wine importers from Kyoto. Mr. Nakamura, plump and loud, and Mr. Togashi, frail and soft-spoken—the Japanese version of Laurel and Hardy—stood politely at the tasting table among the barrels. Candace, the good sommelier and hostess, poured our Albatro—equal parts Merlot and Sangiovese—while delivering her ten learned phrases in

Japanese. Then she added in English, "Let us swirl our wine while my husband brings the *bruschetta,*" and gave me that reassuring smile one saves for ugly babies.

That night I was designated cook. This was a remarkable leap of faith on Candace's part since she is an amazingly inventive chef whereas my repertoire consists of boiled eggs and toast. The fragrance of burning bread greeted me in the kitchen. Eight bits of charcoal smoldered by the fire. The toast was toast.

Ordinarily this is no problem, but we were now in a crisis: those were our last pieces of bread until Friday. Bread is delivered to our door twice a week, when Giuseppe the baker roars up in his tiny van with a mountain of crusty loaves. Acting fast, I scraped away the charcoal until eight communion wafers lay before me. With the gentleness of a brain surgeon, I rubbed garlic on each, then poured on olive oil and ran back to the cellar.

I laid the plate before the wine-swirlers and, to demonstrate, picked up a piece but as I was placing it in my mouth, as if struck by lightning, the paper-thin wafer crumbled in my hand. I licked the oil from my fingertips.

The Japanese are the most polite people on earth—I have seen busloads of them in the gardens of Tokyo form a perfect human square while listening to a tour guide in pouring rain—and now Mr. Nakamura and Mr. Togashi, faithful to their culture, obligingly ate their crumbling wafers, then licked their fingers. "No ploblem," Mr. Nakamura said, and he gracefully reached down and crumbled another.

One course down, two to go.

~

The most vital ingredient in a Tuscan kitchen is wine. Not for cooking, but for drinking while you cook. I uncorked a bottle of our 2002 Merlot, dense and dark and so potent it often has me singing folksongs I didn't know I knew. As it is unfiltered—and to maximize its flavors—I decanted it and poured myself a glass, and then I turned the chicken roasting in a stand-up grill beside the open fire. Chicken turning is not to be taken lightly. I turn it every ten minutes in every way I can: upside down, left to right, from one side of the fire to the other—it helps to have studied the Karma Sutra—to cook each morsel to perfection. Then I began preparing the pasta dish: *fettuccini* with anchovies. I bought the anchovies at the fishmonger's that morning after an elbow-to-elbow battle with a mob of old ladies, with one yelling from the back, "At this rate it would have been faster to go catch it myself."

I pulled the anchovies from their paper, and dumped them in oil with garlic, tomatoes, and parsley. Full of self confidence, I hummed while stirring. When the pasta overflowed I tossed it into the colander. That's when I noticed I forgot to clean the fish. "No plobrem," I mumbled. I speared each little bastard, cut off his head and tail, yanked out his guts, and back he went into the pan.

Nunzi had made the pasta fresh that morning—it was so light it almost fell apart as I put it in the pot—so, left to sit under its own weight in the colander, it took on the consistency of a golf ball. No problem. I reached for a knife. Assuming Mr. Nakamura and Mr. Togashi were new to Tuscan ways, instead of light and fluffy pasta, I served *fettuccini alla cube.*

I heard them coming from the cellar just as the chicken took a dive into the ashes. No problem. I swept it clean with the whiskbroom. They entered, their cheeks rosy and their eyes wandering the kitchen.

The dinner was flawless. The pasta cut effortlessly with steak knives, the ash went down easily with Brunello, and the finale—a fosso-aged *pecorino*—was a perfect mate to a glass of our Syrah.

Afterwards I sat back contentedly and tried to remember their names.

~

With our guests gone, my eyes a bit unfocused, and the full moon shining through the window, I suggested a novelty, a walk through the woods on the new path. Candace looked at me as if I were only a little crazy, which I took to be an enthusiastic yes, until she shook her head as if to clear away the fog.

"It's dark out," she said.

"Not dark, there is a moon."

"There's a moon because it's dark. If it wasn't dark, there'd be the sun."

"Look," I nudged. "This could be one of life's great experiences."

"This could be one of life's *last* experiences."

"Tell you what," I offered. "Let's just start. As soon as you feel uncomfortable we'll turn back."

"I feel uncomfortable. There, I saved you a trip."

But when she saw my disappointment she relented. "Okay Chum," she sighed. "Let's go and play Indiana Jones."

⁓

The moon glowed so bright in the cold night that it made us squint. The shadow of the well loomed like a fallen tower; the branches of the olives were cobwebs against the sky. Only an owl called from somewhere in the vineyard. Through the ilexes and the porcinaio the moonlight streamed into pools on the ground. Then we entered the woods.

"We're on the path," I assured Candace. "Just trust that your feet will always find the ground."

"Until we reach the cliff," Candace sighed.

"The path runs along the cliff, not over it," I argued.

"The path runs along the cliff in daylight. How do I know what paths do at night?"

⁓

I heard her footsteps stop behind me. I turned. She stood there, her face turned up into the light of the moon, eyeing it as she would a rival.

We walked for close to an hour up through the woods, out into the topmost vineyard, and then back past the ruins and down into the canyon. The moonlight danced in the brook. Candace wove her arm into mine and I held her close to keep her warm.

"I feel like we're the last people on earth," she said.

"That would be nice," I said. "Then we'd get to drink all that wine."

37 ~ "A SPELL-CASTING WINE"

*T*he broken peaks of the Dolomites are red in the low sun. Being young mountains, their color is fresh and bright because they crumble faster than they can be weathered grey. To be there in October when the other climbers have gone home is like being alone on the planet.

With the last of the grapes in the cellar, Giancarlo insisted we take a week off. He would happily punch the cap down four times a day, including the goodnight punch at midnight. We packed wine and olive oil and headed for our attic in San Vigilio.

At five thousand feet, the morning air is sharp with frost, so it's best to keep your climbing boots inside at night or you'll think you're sinking your feet straight into ice. We pack light rucksacks for climbing: a thin poncho for rain, a compass, matches, flashlight, altimeter; bread, cheese, and sausages for lunch; and apples, chocolate, and water for short rests. We layer up and wear gloves because at this time of year blizzards have been known to sneak in from the sea. We also take a rope and harness for Buster for where the rock drops sheer.

The first day we climbed up to eight thousand feet to see Rudy, a friend, who looks like a gnome out of some Tyrolean fable. He kept his cows in alpine pastures until the first snowflakes drove them down to the valley for winter. He lived between two small glacial lakes, in a hut, where he happily made us eggs and cheese fresh from his chickens and cows. We ate and drank his beer and left him a bottle of wine. It was nearly dusk by the time we descended from the rocks into the trees.

The next day we climbed high.

As we were leaving the house that morning, Antonio was coming back from the woods with a basket of mushrooms. We told him we were headed for Monte Senes, and he looked up at the clouds flowing past the roof.

"I don't know," he said. "Today it's hard to tell." And he walked away looking unconvinced.

From San Vigilio the road rises to its end in a box canyon where the National Park begins. You can hike the next two thousand feet vertical if you're going no farther, but if you're planning on three thousand more, as we were, it's advisable to call Max from the alpine refuge to take you in his old Land Rover up the torturous trail, leaving you above the tree-line.

~

We came out of the boulders and climbed the edge of a stony meadow. Around us, splintered peaks stood against the sky. There was Monte Cristallo and Croda del Becco, Croda Rossa, Vallon Bianco, and the deadly Cima Nove that took its toll of climbers every year. We bundled up and started toward the peak. Once out of the protection of the boulders, a hard wind lashed our backs.

"Well timed, Chum," Candace said. "Who else could get the wind to blow them to the top?"

Monte Sella di Senes looks formidable from below. The western face is a two-thousand-foot drop without a ledge, while to the south and north are broken ridges, like twisted knives. But to the east, it is climbable without ropes. It just takes a bit of perseverance, with your eyes fixed on the ground, because after the first rise the mountain is fractured, so it's like walking across the ribs of a brontosaurus. The rock here is calcareous, and eons of runoff from glaciers have gouged deep crevices, easy to jump across but just as easy to fall into. I roped Buster in and he beamed, staring bravely at his feet as he leapt. Where the fractures ended, the steep climb began. We followed a mountain goat path with wild-flowers in cracks. Higher up, edelweiss bloomed.

On long climbs, your life flashes with clarity before you. Some say it's the lack of oxygen, others that it's the silence. With the steady climb, I no longer felt the mountain, but rather the stones of the terraces of Syrah.

In the last days of August, before our first harvest, Candace and I went to check the grapes. We began with the top-most terrace. I picked a grape from every fifth vine, always from the same spot on the cluster—about halfway down—then squeezed a drop of juice from it onto the refractometer to measure the sugar. I gave the grape to Candace to taste and to see if the seeds had turned brown, and whether the stem was dark and dry, indicating the end of maturation. The grapes were all showing between 22 and 24 on the scale and tasted sweet with elaborate flavors. We'd been taught not to wait a moment over 24 to avoid high alcohol. We came to where the terrace began to slope; the vines here were weaker, the grapes smaller, the leaves already turning. The scale showed 26, a measure I'd never before seen. Candace bit and spit, then she bit again.

"My God, taste this," she said.

It was like no grape I had tasted. It wasn't just sweeter—there were only a few more percentage points of sugar—but it was more complicated on the pallet: spicier, fruitier, more tannic and entrancing. We tried each vine; the whole row was the same. By accident we had discovered how to make what reviewers would later call a "spell-casting wine."

~

The sky darkened among the peaks to the west, and wisps of clouds lodged in the clefts near us.

We stopped, pulled out our canteens and drank. The fog rolled in except it was no fog: we were being buried by a grey cloud full of snow. Flakes, like butterflies, drifted on the wind.

"Dad! Dad! It's snowing," Buster yelled in glee. "Let's build a snowman."

"We'll soon be snowmen," Candace softly said.

We pushed on through the drifting snow. "I'll leave markers," I said, and gathered rocks to build piles like *mani* stones, the way I had seen done in the mountains of Tibet. To make sure we found the stones on the way back, I made the distance between them the length of Buster's rope. We climbed and built stone piles along the way. The snow blanketed the ground. Candace went ahead. She has the tenacity of a pit bull; even if she hated the climb, she would never want to quit. Five Charlie just keeps flying.

The distant peaks had vanished and only Senes loomed ahead, like some temptress, through the snow. The altimeter said five hundred feet to go. The snow stuck to our wool caps. Behind us the line of *mani* darkened reassuringly in the snow that now smothered the ground. We walked on.

~

The year before, we had harvested the first small crop of Merlot. On a cold morning like this one, it finished fermenting and was ready to be pressed. We fermented in a small wooden barrel, and after we scooped off the wine, there was still half a barrel of soaked grape skins left. Having no press, we ladled the grapes into the stainless steel bucket, sat down on facing benches, and Buster, Candace and I started pressing by hand. We pressed all day, one handful at a time, the wine running through our fingers, dripping into a pail. It was one of the best wines we ever made.

~

We had stopped and dropped our packs in the lee of an outcropping and unwrapped our lunch when the sky went suddenly dark.

"We better pack up," I said.

Candace concurred, packed, and began to climb. I called out for her to stop. She turned around and argued that it would be good to finish, that it would set a good example for Buster for completing a job.

"The mountain will be here tomorrow," I said. She must have sensed from the calm in my voice that it was important to turn back. She looked up at the mountain, lifted her hat, and said, *"A domani,"* until tomorrow.

As we turned into the wind, snowflakes pelted our faces. The snow crunched underfoot as we passed the first *mani*, only its top stone showing. The goat-path in the bluff was protected from the wind but the ribbed rocks below it were too covered with snow to walk safely over them. I pulled out the map to find another way. To the north was an immense and concave cone, an avalanche of scree, which, if we didn't fall, would take us straight down. We pushed through the snow toward it.

~

The day we put on our first labels there had been a light snow. Most wineries use complex machines that label two thousand bottles an hour. We had no machine, so we stuck them on by hand.

It had taken four months and a hundred arguments to decide on a design. We'd tried drawing the house, like the French draw their châteaux; then we tried paintings by Giotto, Lorenzetti and Botticelli; we even tried an old piece of bas-relief from Egypt. But nothing felt right. Then, one winter day, I was writing in the tower when I saw the low sun hit one of Candace's paintings. It lit just a detail but I could not look away. This would be our label.

I took the wooden box of Gaja's Sori San Lorenzo, padded it so the bottle sat high, and drew lines on the sides with a pen to indicate the top of the label. For days Buster, Candace, and I stuck on labels—with the wood box—one bottle at a time.

~

We reached the top of the rise; the cone of scree lay before us. Whipped by the wind, the snow swirled, and once in a while blew apart, like curtains. With the heel of my boot, I gave the scree a try, driving my heel deep through the snow. It held. I tried more gently as if I were someone lighter, like Candace, who might slip, and managed to find hard ground. We retied Buster's rope with him at its center and Candace and me tethered to the ends, we then spread out in a straight line along the cone's rim, and on the count of three, began, one heel at a time, our long and slow decent. We slid and fell, then got up and slid some more. The wind carried Candace and Buster's laughter. I feared they would fall forward and tumble down, but the only threat they seemed to sense was laughing themselves to death. Buster was the first to slalom. We did shallow S's down the hill until one of us would slip and fall, and we'd all tense up and fall down.

The big boulders all around us told us we'd reached bottom. "Let it snow," Buster sang, "let it snow, let it snow."

Josef was at the barn splitting firewood. He stopped when he saw us coming and smiled. I told him about the adventure and finished with our disappointment at turning back a hundred meters from the top. His face went serious. "If it doesn't feel right here," he said, pointing at his stomach. "I've known climbers who'd never turn back." And he nodded toward the mountain. "They're still up there," he said.

38 ~ NEW YEAR'S EVE

By November there was a monastic peace in the cellars. The must had all been pressed; the barrels, filled and bunged, lay in their cradles. Once every two weeks we pulled the big corks and topped off the wine; other than that, the work was done for now.

The *porcini* had come and gone—we'd eaten them grilled, sautéed in garlic, rolled in flour and fried, or spread onto *crostini*, and we still had a stack of them in the freezer.

Buster and I, under the pretense of cutting firewood, were secretly clearing a new Christmas path for Candace. But it wasn't easy: we often had to hide. November is the time for Candace's favorite mushrooms—chanterelles—and she would hunt through our meadows and woods. We'd hear her coming and we'd fall silent and duck down, too often sitting on the thorns we had just cut.

In a clearing beyond the pond, we built a sandstone house with a terracotta roof for chickens and pigeons. Both the fields and woods were full of hens and noisy, prancing roosters, all of them scratching for the best morsels in the ground.

One morning Candace announced a winter outing and we drove up to the volcano. We climbed into woods of tall trees. Beneath them the fallen leaves had been raked and piled, and only little spiny things popped up everywhere. Candace picked one up and held it out toward us. Inside was a dark, shiny bulb.

"*Castagne,*" she said triumphantly, chestnuts. "I'll stuff the goose with these."

The big table was set for Christmas dinner, and in its center was what I had so long dreamed of: bottles of our own wine from vineyards we planted ourselves. The room was alive with a warm feeling of pride and achievement. We had created, against real odds—and most common sense—something that could bring joy to many lives. And the best part of the long adventure was not the wine, or even the accolades, but the precious memories of the people who had worked so hard to help us through the years.

I would gladly trade all the wine in the cellar for more times together.

From the dining room we can look into the kitchen where the fire blazes, or across the courtyard at the Christmas tree lights where the cows slept long ago. To the south through the gazebo are castles, and through the west windows, the vineyards and the hills. The quiet outside seems to have permeated our walls, the stones, the ancient tiles, the beams. And the flavors of the land live in our wines that glow a deep and passionate red in the candlelight.

But perhaps the magic of Tuscany is not all in the senses: not just in its food and wine, or its hill towns, or the drama of its ever-changing light. Perhaps its magic is in the treasure we too often neglect—the peace within ourselves.

New Year's Eve at the ancient hot springs is a night one can't forget.

The village of Bagno Vignoni was built in Roman times, on the side of a gentle hill. To the south a cliff of calcareous rock left by milky, steaming waters, falls to a stream that wanders through a cleft. Across the way the crumbling tower of Rocca D'Orcia hangs above a hamlet bathed in the sun's last rays of the year.

The houses form a ring around an enormous *vasca*, a stone basin, cut into the ground. At dusk, in winter, you can feel the cold air slip down the mountain onto your face and see it mist around the lanterns.

Ancient folklore has it that it's a place where you fall in love. Perhaps it's the warm waters or the mist that rises from them, or the moonlight from the wavelets that dance and shimmer on the walls.

Late one winter night, when the town was asleep, a painter friend was walking home gazing at the moon. Inside the walls of the *vasca*, at the level of the water, are slabs of travertine as benches. She took off her shoes and sat, her feet dangling in the water. No one in sight, she slipped off her clothes and lowered herself into the steam. She swam and felt deliriously happy. When she got back to the bench she found a glass filled with champagne. There was no one around; she toasted the moon. At the far end of the vasca she heard the water move—she turned. A figure slipped in and swam slowly toward her, holding a glass of champagne above the rising steam. She had never seen him before but, face to face, she felt she somehow knew him. They toasted to the stars. And fell in love.

After the tradional *cenone,* an endless dinner that takes up New Year's Eve, the walkway around the *vasca* came alive near midnight. People drifted in wrapped in shawls, carrying bags of fireworks, candles, and champagne. They set up the candles on the stone rim and attached their fireworks to boards, railings, or branches.

The clusters of candles swelled and voices, at first muffled in the moist air, grew louder. Just before midnight, the windows above a long stairway swung open into the moonlight. We didn't see who actually gave the signal, but champagne corks popped, the wicks of fireworks sizzled, and through the windows Verdi's *"Nessun dorma"* drifted out into the night. From all around the *vasca* fireworks burst and streaked across the sky, lighting up walls and rooftops, chimneys, statues, clinking glasses, and smiling faces.

And I kissed my nearest and dearest, and hoped no one would pinch me and wake me from the dream.

We set the fireworks—pinwheels and a starburst—on the *vasca*'s edge, and Candace stuck a silver rocket into a stone's crack, but bent the wire so it pointed at the bright orb in the sky.

She smiled. "What do you say we shoot for the moon."

ACKNOWLEDGMENTS

*T*his book would not exist without the care and dedication of friends from Tuscany to New York. To Piccardi and the masons of Pignatai: Fosco, Piero, Georgi, Alessandro, Arnaldo, and Asea; and the other master craftsmen: Mario, Scarpini, Enzo, and Marco: thank you for helping us rebuild Colombaio with unremitting hard work and pride, creating a thing of beauty that will stand for centuries. To our advisors: Fabrizio, Guillaume, and Oriano; and the machine operators who virtually sculpted the land: Rino and Constantino: thank you for bringing the abandoned lands to life. To Giancarlo, Alfiero, Alessandro, Gianni, Pelo, Vasco, and the two Nunzis: thank you for planting the vines and tending them with love over the years. And our gratitude to those who helped us make the wine: the brilliant consultants Carlo Corino and Roberto Cipresso.

Thanks to my associate Céline Little, who skillfully edited

jumbled memories, and with her dry humor kept us laughing all the while. And, as always, there was Norton's Editor-in-Chief, my dear pal, Starling Lawrence, who, with the sacrifices he has made, must be gunning for sainthood.

Candace was the best partner one could ask for: friend, psychologist, architect, carpenter, and, finally, winemaker who magically turned the grapes into ambrosia. Above every-thing, I thank our beloved son, Peter, who not only actively helped from age five, but also gave a reason for it all.

It was a true joy and an honor working with every one of you.

THE MÁTÉ WINE ESTATE

*T*he Máté family wine estate nestles on two private hills in the temperate, seaward zone of Montalcino. A Roman vineyard 2,000 year ago, the seven *campi* of marvelously-varied terrior lie between 900 and 1200 feet above sea level. Totaling 15.75 acres among Mediterranean woods of herbs and wild fruit, they were designed by Fabrizio Moltard, agronomist to Angelo Gaja. The clones, chosen for each field by France's Pierre Guillaume, comprise: Sangiovese (in fossil-filled tuffo), Merlot (in sandy clay), Cabernet Sauvignon (in galestro), and Syrah (on mineral-rich, southern terraces).

Planted to a high density of 3,000 vines per acre, the yields are kept extremely low by three annual green prunings to concentrate flavors. Selected, hand-picked at fullest maturity and fermented in small temperature-controlled stainless steel vats or new wooden barrels, the grapes are punched down by hand to extract color and tannins, while the must is kept cool to maintain the rich aromas of fruit and spices.

The wines are aged for up to two and a half years in Allier French oak *barriques* and *tonneaux*. The total annual production is 25,000 bottles.

Total acres of land	- 70
Total acres planted to vines	- 15.75
Sangiovese	- 10.6
Merlot	- 2.5
Cabernet Sauvignon	- 1.75
Syrah	- .9

www.matewine.com   www.ferencmate.com

MÁTÉ WINE REVIEWS AND RATINGS

Brunello di Montalcino (100% Sangiovese)

Wine Spectator	**90**
Decantor (Steven Spurrier)	★★★★

Loads of blackberry, tobacco and light vanilla follow through to a full-bodied palate, with good fruit and a silky, refined finish. Lots of sweet, ripe flavors.   *—James Suckling*

Very dark crimson. Big mouthful of fruit hits the palate and there's a certain delicacy. ***Really* distinctive!**

—Jancis Robinson

Banditone (100% Syrah)

Wine Spectator	**92**
Boston Globe/winereviewonline	**92**
Gerhard Eichelmann's *Mondo*	**90**
Morrell/New York ***100 Best Wines of 2007***	
Great Italian Reds **#1**	

Offers rich plum and black pepper character on the nose. Full-bodied, with velvety tannins and a long finish. Caressing and pretty. Hard to resist now.   *—James Suckling*

"Pure Northern Rhone."   *—Steven Spurrier*

Banditone (100% Syrah) cont'd

Luscious. Gorgeously layered with seductive-ripe black fruit
and plum-like flavors. —*Dr. Michael Apstein*

Mantus (100% Merlot)

Wine Spectator	**91**
Wine & Spirits	**90**

Aromas of plum, blackberry and chocolate. Full-bodied with
velvety tannins and a long, long finish. Delicious.
—*James Suckling*

Albatro (Sangiovese/Merlot/Cab)

Wine & Spirits	**91**
Wine Spectator	**88**

Displays aromas of ripe fruit and fresh rosemary. Full-bodied,
with a silky mouthfeel. Shows complexity and structure.
—*James Suckling*

Cabernet Sauvignon (100%)

Wine Spectator	(not yet reviewed)
Luca Maroni	*I Migliori Vini Italiani 2008*
	The Best Italian Wines 2008

CLASSIC TUSCAN RECIPES
from Trattoria Castello Banfi

Almost every big meal in Tuscany begins with a selection of toasted bread topped with delicious seasonal spreads—in spring centered on fresh vegetables, in winter reverting to such staples as liver spread and lard with sausage, and in December based on the simplicity of the peppery new olive oil. *Bruschetta* refers to a slice of regular Tuscan bread, toasted, rubbed with garlic, anointed with olive oil, and topped with whatever is handy, such as chopped liver, or sausage bits, or tomato.

Crostini are small rounds from a *frusta*, or baguette-like long, thin bread, toasted and topped generally with more spreadable concoctions like olive paste or goat cheese. Perhaps *bruschetta* is more rustic and crostini are more refined, but both are delicious-and their variations are endless.

Bruschetta al Olio Nuovo

What better comfort to winter's dreary cold than fresh Tuscan bread toasted on an open flame, gently rubbed with garlic and coated with peppery and fruity freshly-pressed olive oil?

Bruschetta al Cavolfiore

1 cauliflower head
1 garlic clove
extra virgin olive oil
salt & pepper to taste

Remove the large leaves from the cauliflower head and boil it in salted water—careful not to overcook to the point that it falls apart. Remove from water, drain, and break into pieces to be placed on top of sliced bread that has previously been toasted and rubbed with garlic. Douse generously with olive oil, and sprinkle with salt and abundant black pepper. Optional: you can also sprinkle on some peperoncini.

Bruschetta or Crostini al Fegatini

1 lb chicken liver
1 lb ground veal
1/2 veal spleen
1 bunch of parsley, cut

1 medium onion, finely chopped
2-3 tsp tomato concentrate
chopped capers
anchovy paste or finely chopped anchovy

Sauté the parsley and onion in olive oil. When the onion is golden, add the ground veal and cook until browned. Boil the liver separately for a few minutes, then mix with the cooked ground veal and the spleen in a blender to a spreadable consistency. Return to the frying pan and brown again, adding a splash of white wine. Stir in the tomato concentrate (after having dissolved it in a bit of warm water), the capers, and the anchovies, and finish cooking for 1 to 2 more minutes.

Crostini agli Asparagi

2 lbs asparagus, snapped and finely diced
1/4 c heavy cream
olive oil and butter for frying
warm water
salt & pepper to taste

Fry the asparagus in butter and olive oil. Add some warm water to soften, then season with salt and pepper. Once the asparagus is tender, add cream and then mash the asparagus with a fork to a spreadable consistency.

Zuppa di Farro (Ristorante Boccon di Vino, Montalcino)

32 oz. fresh or dried cannelloni beans
12 oz. fresh or dried chickpeas
12 oz. pearled spelt barley
7 oz. bacon, chopped into bits
12 c vegetable broth
garlic (minced)
onion (diced)
salt & peperoncini to taste
tomato concentrate
extra virgin olive oil

If using dried beans and chickpeas, soak them the day before. Mash one third of the cannelloni beans. Gently fry the onions and garlic in the olive oil until the onion is translucent, then add all the chickpeas, the mashed cannelloni, and 1/2 of the remaining whole cannelloni beans, and simmer for a few minutes. Add a dash of the tomato concentrate and blend in the broth. Separately, fry the bacon bits and add them to the soup along with the peperoncini and salt. Boil for about 40 minutes, stirring frequently to be sure that the soup does not stick to the bottom of the pot. Add the remaining cannelloni beans and the pearled spelt barley and boil for 20 more minutes. Serve hot in a bowl over a slice of toasted Tuscan bread and drizzle some fresh extra virgin olive oil on top. Serves 50.

Arista Al Forno

Legend has it that this boneless pork roast got the name "Arista," a word used exclusively in Tuscany, when the Archduke of Tuscany held a banquet at which the Greek Patriarch was in attendance. After being served this dish, he exclaimed his delight with the Greek term "aristos," a praise of the highest caliber. The Tuscans mangled the pronunciation a bit, but the meaning is there, and the dish is truly exalted!

4 sage leaves
4 rosemary sprigs
Peel of 1/4 lemon
Pinch of fine salt and freshly ground black pepper
1 boneless pork loin (1 1/2 lbs to 1 3/4 lbs)
2-3 tbsp extra virgin olive oil
2 garlic cloves
6 oz white wine

Finely chop the sage, garlic, rosemary, and lemon peel, mix with the salt and pepper, and rub the herbs into the meat. Place the roast in a baking pan with the olive oil (coat the pan and sprinkle some on top of the roast) and cook for about 1 1/2 hours at 325°F. Turn the roast and pour the wine over it. Increase temperature to 425°F until the alcohol evaporates. Remove from the oven and let sit for a few minutes before slicing and serving with its juices. Serves 5.

Cinghiale in Scottiglia

The Tuscan countryside is rich with various types of game and poultry, so the *scottiglia* method of stewing probably originated in this part of Italy. Different types of meat can be prepared *in scottiglia*, including chicken, guinea hen, rabbit, lamb, pheasant, and wild boar. The method is the same for all with the exception of wild boar, which must be marinated overnight because of its gamy character, first browned on its own to remove excess liquid from the marinade and then finished with the addition of a small amount of milk. The following recipe for wild boar in scottiglia can be adapted to other meats by skipping those three steps.

1 lb wild boar, cut into small pieces
10 1/2 oz extra virgin olive oil
aromatic herbs: 3 garlic cloves, 3 medium-sized carrots, 2 stalks celery, and 1 medium onion, finely chopped
a few sprigs of sage, rosemary, and parsley, and a few whole bay leaves
salt, black pepper, and peperoncini to taste
1/3 c whole milk
10 oz peeled or fresh tomatoes
1 bottle Brunello di Montalcino

Soak the meat overnight in a marinade composed of 1/4 bottle of wine, 3 1/2 oz water, and one third of the aromatic herbs. Remove the meat from the marinade and place it in a frying pan with another third of the aromatic herbs (but no oil) and a tablespoon of salt, and cook over a medium flame, allowing the liquids from the marinade to "sweat out" of the meat (about 10 minutes).

Remove the meat from the pan and place in a clean pan with olive oil. Gently brown, then add the remaining aromatic herbs, peperoncini, and salt and black pepper to taste. Continue cooking a few minutes more, then add an abundant glass or two of Brunello, leaving to simmer until the alcohol evaporates. Finally, add the tomatoes and cook until a dense sauce is formed. Finish by adding the milk in the last few minutes of cooking. Serves 4.

Bisteca Fiorentina

Roasted over the dried vineyard cuttings and anointed simply with extra virgin olive oil, what else could be at one time so simple and yet so regal as this T-bone steak?

Insalata di Farro (Ristorante Boccon di Vino, Montalcino)

2 1/4 lbs hulled spelt
3 1/3 lbs frozen green beans
2 1/4 lbs baby shrimp
1 bunch chives cut to 1/2-in pieces
salt, pepper & aromatic herbs to taste
extra virgin olive oil

Cook the spelt (like rice) in salted boiling water for 20-25 minutes and then let cool. Cook the green beans in salted boiling water, immersed while frozen to maintain their color, then drain and chop. If the baby shrimp are frozen, immerse in boiling water for a moment, then cover with cold water. Mix the spelt, shrimp, beans and chives with olive oil, salt, pepper, and aromatic herbs, and serve at room temperature with a drop of olive oil. Serves 5.

Vegetable Purée

8 1/2 oz lentils
8 1/2 oz chick peas
8 1/2 oz cannelloni beans
salt, extra virgin olive oil, and tomato concentrate to taste
2 garlic cloves
2 sprigs fresh rosemary
1 peperoncino
bacon for garnish

Boil and then drain the vegetables; meanwhile, fry the garlic, rosemary, and some of the peperoncino in the olive oil and then add the vegetables with a bit of their water. Add salt to taste and tomato concentrate for a touch of color. Pass through a food mill and add a bit of oil. Serve on top of toasted bread slices with a piece of bacon on each. Serves 10.

Fiori di Zucca Fritti (Fried zucchini flower)

1/2 c flour
1 tbsp "extra virgin" olive oil
1/2 c soft breadcrumbs
1 c milk
20 zucchini flowers, still closed
5 anchovy fillets
1 tbsp chopped parsley
salsa balsamica Etrusca (Castello Banfi)
salt and pepper to taste

Combine flour and oil with enough water to obtain a pasty batter. Soak the breadcrumbs in the milk and strain them. Shorten the stem of the zucchini flowers, take out the pistil, and stuff them with the breadcrumbs mixed with the anchovy fillets and parsley. Coat the flowers with batter and fry in boiling oil. Season with salt and pepper. Drain on kitchen towel. Sprinkle generously with salsa balsamica and serve immediately, hot and crispy. Serves 4.

Salsa Balsamica Etrusca in Cuisine

When cooking with balsamica, here are two points to remember:
1. It is naturally very "individualist" (it easily overpowers other condiments), and on cooked foods, tradition usually calls for Balsamica last in the sequence of a recipe's ingredients.

2. Balsamica enhances the flavors of the single ingredients.

I Sapori del Castellano (the lord of the castle's dressing)

1 tbsp salsa balsamica Etrusca
3 tbsp "extra virgin" olive oil
1 tsp olive pâté

Mix the three ingredients in a terracotta bowl. Stir with a wooden spoon until smoothly blended. Combine with vegetables just before serving. Recommended as a vegetable dip and as a dressing for green and mixed salads, mushroom salads, and vegetable salads.